THE
GREATEST
PSYCHOLOGIST
WHO EVER
LIVED

THE GREATEST PSYCHOLOGIST WHO EVER LIVED

Jesus and the Wisdom of the Soul

MARK W. BAKER, PH.D.

HarperSanFrancisco
A Division of HarperCollinsPublishers

HarperCollins Web site: http://www.harpercollins.com
HarperCollins®, ☕®, and HarperSanFrancisco™ are trademarks of
HarperCollins Publishers, Inc.

FIRST EDITION
Designed by Joseph Rutt

Library of Congress Cataloging-in-Publication Data
Baker, Mark W., Ph.D.
The greatest psychologist who ever lived : Jesus and
the wisdom of the soul / Mark W. Baker.—1st ed.
p. cm.
Includes bibliographical references.
ISBN 0–06–067088–6 (cloth)
ISBN 0–06–067087–8 (pbk.)
1. Jesus Christ—Teachings. 2. Jesus Christ—Psychology. I. Title.
BS2415.B325 2000
232.9'03—dc21   00–063373
01 02 03 04 05 ❖/RRD(H) 10 9 8 7 6 5 4 3 2 1

Contents

ACKNOWLEDGMENTS

Everything I do is the product of the relationships I have with others. This book is no exception. I want to thank my wife, Barbara, and my son, Brendan, for enduring the birth of this book with me. I must thank J. D. Hinton and Gary Verboon for helping me focus on the goal of writing, as only good friends can. Thank you to Mimi Craven for her photographic expertise. Thanks to Carmen Berry, Thereza Verboon, Dr. Don and Simone Morgan, Tim and Joan Swift, Dwight and Virginia Case, Eugene and Virginia Lowe, Michael and Lorraine Chapman, Dr. Peter and Kary Radestock, Dr. Lynn Becker, Dr. Dan Spector, and Madison and Linda Mason for being the kind of friends who have transformed me. Thank you to Dr. Scott Weimer, Dr. Mack Harnden, Dr. Steve Murray, Dr. Joe Venema, Dr. Walt and Fran Becker, and Ellen Rhoda for shaping my spiritual life over the years.

I am grateful to all of my patients, both past and present, who have taught me so much about people. I am grateful to Dr. Robert Stolorow, who taught me how to think about therapy. I am thankful for my friends and colleagues at the La Vie Counseling Center, especially Jeanie Price, Greta Hassel, Clint Daniels, Dr. Curtis Miller, and Dr. Jim Bickley, who contributed to the ideas here along with Janet Joslyn and Dr. Alan Karlbelnig. I am also thankful for Dennis Palumbo, Dr. Bruce Howard, Micki Alter, Dr. Elisabeth Crim, Dr. Rob Piehl, and Dr. Craig Wagner, who have inspired me to understand my patients with greater skill than I could have achieved on my own. I am grateful to Dr. Howard Bacal for the depth of his impact upon me personally.

I also want to thank my parents, Charles and Diane Baker, and my siblings, Tim, Paula, Mitch, Phillip, and Lisa, for shaping my early years and encouraging me to study psychology. Thank you to the spiritual communities at Westwood Presbyterian Church and Brentwood Presbyterian Church for giving me safe places to put together ideas about psychology and theology. And I am especially grateful for Julie Castiglia of the Castiglia Literary Agency and Gideon Weil and John Loudon of Harper San Francisco for having the vision to grasp this book as an idea and help transform it into written form.

INTRODUCTION

Jesus understood people. We know this because he is arguably the most influential person in all of history. Cultures have been shaped, wars fought, and individual lives transformed as a result of his itinerant ministry two thousand years ago. As a psychologist, I am fascinated with the question of why his teachings were so powerful. After years of study, I have found that a psychological understanding of the teachings of Jesus helps us understand why his words had such a profound impact upon his followers. Given the knowledge we have of psychological theories today, I believe we can see how Jesus' psychologically brilliant grasp of people made them want to listen to him.

For over twenty years I have been interested in the study of both theology and psychology. I have found each discipline helps to deepen my understanding of the other. I have never ceased to be amazed at the points of agreement between spiritual and emotional principles that facilitate health.

Freud however, considered religion a crutch people used to deal with their feelings of helplessness. This started a war between psychology and religion that continues to this day. Some psychologists view religion as a cult that limits human potential, and some religious people view psychology as a cult for the very same reason. I have found the animosity existing on both sides of this conflict to be rooted in fear. Fear inhibits understanding. It is only when people stop being threatened long enough to listen to each other that they can begin to truly comprehend each other.

Years ago I was asked by a colleague to take a speaking engagement he was unable to keep the next Sunday at a church. Although I didn't know anything about the church, I agreed to give one of my talks on a psychologically relevant subject geared to a religious audience. Several minutes into my lecture a man in the back of the room raised his hand and said, "This might be an interesting seminar for a Tuesday night at the library or something, but it doesn't belong in the House of God on the Lord's Day!" Needless to say, it was a tough room. Unfortunately, this was neither the first nor the last time I have encountered such a hostile attitude toward "secular psychology" by certain religious people.

But both sides of the conflict support this antipathy. Once, after a series of difficult conversations with a group of psychoanalysts on the subject of Christianity, I discussed my disappointment over what appeared to be their prejudice toward religious people with another psychoanalyst friend of mine. His explanation for their behavior was, "I am familiar with those men, and I don't think they know personally any therapist who is both intelligent and Christian." Those psychoanalysts were just as guilty of holding prejudices against religious people, whom they had excluded from their professional lives, as the religious people who didn't want psychology to be allowed into their religious lives.

Fortunately Freud did not have the final say on either religion or psychology. Contemporary psychologists are reevaluating many of Freud's ideas, and it's time to include his prejudice against religion in that process. For several years, I have been very excited about the advancements in the field of psychology. The points of agreement between contemporary theories and the ancient teachings of Jesus have astonished me.

Jesus taught through the subjective style of telling parables; we now have the psychoanalytic theories of intersubjectivity to explain why. Jesus believed a relationship with God was the source of salvation; the relational schools of psychoanalysis clarify why this makes psychological sense. Jesus did not see himself as existing apart from Someone outside of himself; psychological theories are saying similar things about the existence of the "self." Jesus welcomed childlike feelings; psychological theories of affect explain why. Jesus understood how the mind could be divided against itself; we now understand how the unconscious can battle with the conscious. Jesus saw sin as broken relationship with God; psychopathology results from ruptures in relationships according to contemporary theories. What Jesus called idolatry psychologists call addiction. Jesus taught we must know and be known by God; therapy heals through empathy. Jesus explained righteousness through a vertical relationship with God; psychologists explain mental health through horizontal relationships between people. And this is just a beginning.

Many books have already been written on the teachings of Jesus. Most of us are familiar with the traditional interpretations of what he had to say, but I would like to add some new reflections on this ancient wisdom. My study of contemporary psychoanalytic theories has allowed me to understand the teachings of Jesus in a different light and has enriched my life and the lives of my patients. Rather than finding the teachings of Jesus contradicted by these new psychological developments, I have found them illuminated, producing profound psychological insights I had not understood before. Let us take a fresh look at some well-known sayings to learn something new about the wisdom of Jesus in light of contemporary psychological thought.

Each of the following chapters centers on a psychoanalytic concept that I will be illustrating with the teachings of Jesus. I have made references in footnotes for those who wish to read technical psychoanalytic writings about them. I have endeavored to spell out these complicated concepts in simple terms without sacrificing the integrity of their meaning. My goal was to avoid sacrificing either simplicity or integrity, even though at moments this seemed impossible to do.

I believe a number of spiritual principles in the teachings of Jesus benefit us in our attempts to live psychologically healthy lives. I would like to give examples how these spiritual principles apply to the lives of people today. The examples I will be using have been taken from the lives of people I have worked with, known, or read about. For reasons of confidentiality, each example is actually a composite of several people and does not represent any one individual person. Unless otherwise noted, I quote Jesus from the New International Version of the Bible. Independent of the personal religious or psychological beliefs we might hold, we can all benefit from timeless wisdom.

PART 1

UNDERSTANDING PEOPLE

CHAPTER 1

UNDERSTANDING HOW PEOPLE THINK

"What shall we say the kingdom of God is like, or what parable shall we use to describe it? It is like a mustard seed, which is the smallest seed you plant in the ground. Yet when planted, it grows and becomes the largest of all garden plants, with such big branches that the birds of the air can perch in its shade."

With many similar parables Jesus spoke the word to them, as much as they could understand. He did not say anything to them without using a parable.

Mark 4:30–34

Life is about faith. Jesus knew that most of what we do in life is simply taken on faith. We like to think we are rational beings living logical lives based upon facts. But the truth is, we are rationalizing beings who base most of our decisions on what we feel or believe and come up with the logic afterwards to justify our decisions. Jesus used parables to force us to deal with what we believe rather than what we think we know. He understood that people like to think they know more than they really do.

Because we don't know as much as we think we do, the truly knowledgeable person is always humble. Jesus never wrote a book, always spoke in parables, and led people to the truth through his living example. He was confident without being arrogant, believed in absolutes without being rigid, and was clear about his own identity without being judgmental toward others.

Jesus approached people with psychological skills that we are just beginning to understand. Instead of giving scholarly lectures based upon his theological knowledge, he humbly made his points through simple stories. He didn't use his knowledge to *talk down* to people; he used a humble means of communication to talk *with* them. He spoke in a manner that made people listen because he knew what made them want to listen. I believe Jesus was a powerful communicator because he understood what the science of psychology is teaching us today—that we base our lives more on what we believe than on what we actually know.

His harshest criticisms were leveled at religious teachers, yet he was one himself. You see, he did not criticize them for their knowledge, but rather for their arrogance. To him, knowledge becomes toxic when people cease to be teachable. The more we learn, the more we should realize how much there is that we don't yet know. Arrogance is a sign of insecurity and only proves a lack of self-knowledge on the part of those who display it. Jesus understood that human ideas are crude approximations of the universe—his psychologically brilliant teaching style always took this into account. I believe we need to learn what Jesus knew about the relationship between knowledge and humility if *we* want to be more effective communicators.[1] Truly great thinkers are humble about what they know. They realize life isn't as much about knowledge as it is about faith.

WHY JESUS SPOKE IN PARABLES

He did not say anything to them without using a parable.
Mark 4:34

Jesus understood how people think. He was one of the greatest teachers in history because he knew that each person can only understand things from his or her own perspective. Because he did not assume that what he had to say would always be understood, he taught in parables.

A parable is an insight into reality in story form. People can take from a parable whatever truths they are able to grasp and begin applying them in their lives. As they grow and evolve, they can return to the parable to extract additional meanings to guide them further along their path.

Parables have helped me understand life. This was especially true during one of my most difficult periods, when I was having trouble making sense out of my suffering. It was one of those times when I was forced to question everything, you know, the how-can-there-be-a-God-if-I-am-suffering kind of period. I was in despair, and nothing was helping.

During this time, I went over to my brother's house to bemoan my situation. Tim is a geologist who spends most of his days outdoors. He doesn't say much, but when he does, it's usually pretty good. I have always considered him to be a humble man, in the best sense of the word.

I was sitting in his kitchen looking depressed and feeling hopeless when he said, "You know, Mark, when I was out doing a geological survey recently, I noticed an interesting thing about the way the world is made. Our team climbed up to the tallest mountain in the area, and we were exhilarated by the view. Mountaintop experiences are great. However, when you are up that high you are above the timberline. You see trees only up to a certain altitude, and above that they can't survive. On the very top of the mountain there is no growth. But if you look down you notice an interesting thing. All the growth is in the valleys."

The meaning I took away from Tim's parable was that suffering feels bad, but it can also lead to growth. It's important to make sense out of things, and that parable helped me do that. I'll never forget what Tim said that day. It didn't take my pain away, but somehow it made it more tolerable.

Parables don't change the facts of our lives—they help us change our perspectives on them. Because each of us can only understand things from our own perspective, Jesus used parables to help us where we need it most. Most of the time we can't change the facts in our lives, but we can change our perspective.

SPIRITUAL PRINCIPLE: We can only understand things from our own perspective.

HOW WE KNOW THE TRUTH

"I am the way and the truth and the life."
John 14:6

Don came to his first therapy session with a list. He didn't like to waste time, and since therapy is expensive, he wanted to present me with the problems he was facing in his life and get my advice on how he should go about solving them.

Even though I like to give advice to people when I am not doing therapy, I saw early on that this was not what Don needed from me. He was under the impression that if he could just acquire the right kind of information, he could fix whatever was wrong in his life. It has been my experience that most people already have more knowledge than they are able to apply in their lives, and perhaps that is the reason they come to therapy.

When we came to the end of one session, Don asked me for some homework in order to make use of our time even between sessions.

"I'm not going to give you any homework," I said.

"Why not?" he asked.

"Because that will only prove that you are the kind of guy who does homework, and we already know that. You are here to learn something new about yourself. I think you will use homework to put more things in your head, when what we need to do is get more things out of your heart."

Gradually Don's life began to change in spite of the fact that he got very little advice from me. What he did get from me was a different kind of relationship from others he had in his life. He started to focus less on what I thought about things and more on how he felt about them. As he became better able to trust his relationship with me, he found himself delving into areas of his life he had never explored before. The more he learned about himself, the better able he was to see why he made the decisions he did in his life. Don came to the most important truths about his life not because of my advice, but because our relationship was one that could guide him to a deeper understanding of himself.

Jesus knew that people using their intellect alone could never come to a complete understanding of the truth about life. He didn't say, "Let me teach you about the truth"; he said, "I am the truth." He knew that the highest form of knowledge comes from trusting relationships rather than greater amounts of information. He answered direct questions with metaphors to invite listeners into a dialogue and into a relationship with him.

This spiritual principle, that we learn the deepest truths in life through our relationships, is the basis for how I do therapy. We all have conscious and unconscious[2] ideas that affect our perception of things. This is why we can only know the truth from our own perspective. It is psychologically impossible to *completely* set aside the influences of our own minds on the way we perceive things. This is especially so because we are unaware of them most of the time. Consequently, everything we think we know intellectually is filtered through what we already believe. Therapy provides people with a relationship that can lead to a greater understanding of themselves and consequently every other truth in their lives.

SPIRITUAL PRINCIPLE: We learn the deepest truths through our relationships.

WHY WE TRY TO BE OBJECTIVE

"But wisdom is proved right by her actions."
Matthew 11:19

Craig and Betty had similar values and goals in life that made them a good match, and their marriage worked rather well for the first several years. However, Betty gradually became dissatisfied with their relationship. She rarely felt she got anywhere when she first tried to talk to Craig about her fears concerning their marriage, and she had given up trying to argue with him because their fights almost always ended leaving her feeling she was simply wrong about the cause of the disagreement. Betty respected Craig, but lately she didn't feel safe enough to even bring up her fears with him, and that bothered her terribly.

"I've never been unfaithful to you, and I've always been a good provider for you and the kids. I just don't think it's right for you to be afraid. If you would just look at things objectively, you'd see we have a good marriage," Craig insisted.

"This isn't about who's right and who's wrong," Betty replied. "It's about feeling safe enough to say how I feel."

"Safe?" Craig asked. "You're not looking at the facts! You have a nice house, a savings account, and a million-dollar life insurance policy on me. The only way you would be more safe would be if I died."

Conversations like this never helped Betty much.

It was not until after they came for marriage counseling that Betty started to feel differently about their marriage. Craig began to realize that the objective facts he was trying to get Betty to look at weren't helping her. She didn't want to argue with Craig about the irrationality of her fears; she wanted him to understand that she was afraid anyway and needed support. She wasn't telling him about her fears so he could fix them; she was sharing her vulnerable feelings in hopes that she could feel closer to him.

Craig's attempts to be objective were only helping him feel better about his role as a husband; that approach gave him something to do that he understood. Craig felt better looking at the facts. The problem was that it wasn't helping Betty. She just needed him to listen and respond with compassion. There is a time when being objective about the facts misses the point. Once Craig became aware of this, he was better able to respond to Betty in a manner that was really helpful to her.

People tend to deify objectivity. We say things like, "Just give me the facts," as if getting the facts were really the most important thing to do. Conclusions based upon objective facts give us a sense of security. We can then turn our attention to the business of daily living without having to spend time and energy contemplating the matters we have resolved. But to Jesus *wisdom* was much more important than amassing objective facts. To him, the application of knowledge in our relationships was much more important than the acquisition of it in our heads. This is what he meant when he said, "Wisdom is proved right by her actions." We can be objectively right about something that has devastating consequences in our relationships with others, but wisdom always considers the consequences of our actions.

Jesus taught that insisting that we have arrived at the objective facts on things can be dangerous at times. Wars have been fought, religions split, marriages ended, children disowned, and friendships dissolved because of it. Sometimes winning arguments can cost us relationships. As the old saying goes, in marriage you have two choices: you can be right, or you can be happy.

SPIRITUAL PRINCIPLE: Seek wisdom more than knowledge.

YOU CAN BE SINCERELY WRONG

"Humble men are very fortunate!"
Matthew 5:3 (Living Bible)

Sometimes we place great confidence in what we think because it gives us a sense of false security. We may sincerely believe that something is true, but we can be sincerely wrong.[3] Jesus warned us to not mistake sincerity for truth. None of us believe what we believe because we think it is false. We believe it because we maintain it is true. Jesus taught that we should be humble about what we think we know, because we can only know the truth from our own perspective.

Back when I was in college, one group of counterculture Christians used to place a preacher on one of the densely populated corners on campus to take advantage of the captive audience that could be found there. I came to know one student-preacher whom I regularly passed as he preached the message of Jesus with all of his strength. I was impressed with his sincerity and the strength of his convictions. Because of the confident manner in which he portrayed himself and because of the fact that he kept doing it for months, I was sure he must have been effective in converting others to his group. I finally stopped him one day after one of his sermons and asked him, "So how many people have you guys seen come to Christ because of your street ministry?" To my surprise his response was, "None actually. But that doesn't matter. This is our calling anyway."

He absolutely believed he was doing the right thing. The outcome was not as crucial as the sincerity with which he was pursuing the task. I never doubted his genuineness, but I did question whether he was right about his calling. Just because he was sincere didn't make him right. Actually, I was aware of dozens of college students who were offended by his preaching and who were less interested in the God he was preaching about because they didn't want to identify with someone they viewed as so oblivious to others. Their impression was that he was making God out to be irrelevant to their daily lives. His goal couldn't have been more the opposite.

My friend the preacher had missed an important truth about life that Jesus would have wanted him to know. It requires great strength of character to be a person of strong conviction and considerable flexibility at the same time. Psychologically mature people can be courageous enough to be sincerely committed to the truth about something and yet remain open to the possibility of being sincerely wrong about how they perceive it. This is the relationship between knowledge and humility.

Jesus said, "Humble men are very fortunate," because rigidity hurts the one being rigid the most. He knew that pretending to have all the answers leads to misfortune, because despite our good intentions we can still be sincerely wrong.

SPIRITUAL PRINCIPLE: Don't mistake sincerity for truth; you can be sincerely wrong.

DON'T CONDEMN WHAT YOU DON'T UNDERSTAND

"Do not condemn, and you will not be condemned."
Luke 6:37

There is an old story about three blind men who encountered an elephant. When asked to describe the elephant, each one said something different. One said the elephant was like a big water hose; the second said it was like a broomstick; and the third said it was like a tree trunk. Each described what he felt from his own perspective. None of them was right or wrong; they all were only speaking from their own perspectives. It is humbling to realize that we are all like the blind men, each limited in our ability to perceive the things that are right in front of us.

Luke and Annie came for marriage counseling because of an impasse they had reached in their relationship. Annie was a conservative person with a few close friends with whom she shared her deepest feelings. Luke was an outspoken, successful businessman who cared for his family and was a committed husband and father.

Although we encountered several problems in our work together, the biggest problem Luke had with Annie was that he saw her as "too emotional." Every time they would get into a disagreement, she would cry or get her feelings hurt, and Luke would fly into a rage, complaining that she refused to be "rational" about things. By the time they came for therapy, their relationship had polarized them into two extremes. Luke was the cold and rational one, and Annie was the overemotional one. People often become a more extreme version of what they started out to be in their marriage as a result of their partner's reactions.

Luke was raised to do the right thing no matter what he felt about it. Being right came first; feelings were always second.

Because of this, he never allowed himself to experience his feelings fully. Being reliable was important; feelings just got in the way.

Because it was so easy for Annie to express her feelings, Luke was constantly being thrown off balance. Over the years, he had come to fear Annie's feelings because he didn't know how to respond to them in a helpful way. We fear what we don't know. "Oh, no. Here you go again!" he would wail, whenever she got in touch with how things felt. The whole area of feelings was a big unknown for Luke. As a result, he feared intense emotions and was very judgmental toward people who displayed them.

"I don't give a flip about how you feel about it. Just do it," he would say. Of course, Annie would only get more emotional in response to this, which made things worse.

Things started to get better for Luke and Annie when they came to the realization that they were both condemning Annie for having feelings. Luke's response to Annie changed when he realized that he was judging feelings to be bad because he didn't understand them. He came to understand that feelings are not good or bad; they are just another source of information needed to make a marriage work. Perhaps there could be something helpful about listening to how Annie felt. Luke helped his marriage get better when he stopped being so certain that Annie was *too* emotional and started trying to see things from her perspective.

This helped Annie to stop condemning herself for having such intense emotional reactions to things. She wasn't "overemotional." She was just someone who felt bad about being emotional, which caused her to spiral down every time she got upset. Allowing herself to have feelings enabled them to come and go more naturally. Luke and Annie still have arguments, but they get through them much faster now. Afterwards Luke often says, "You know, I'm glad we talked about this." Luke and Annie have taken the sting out of their fighting by realizing that condemning

Annie for being emotional was based upon a misunderstanding of her reaction.

Jesus warned us about the pitfalls of judging others. He knew that whatever we were basing our judgments on was information that was colored by our own biases and not complete enough to render us any kind of absolute authority. This makes many of us feel insecure. We want to believe that we know the complete truth about things so we can feel safe in the knowledge that nothing new will come up to throw us off balance. This fear of the unknown is the basis for intolerance. It makes us become judgmental in our thinking. When we are afraid in this way, we condemn what we don't understand.

SPIRITUAL PRINCIPLE: In judging others, we condemn ourselves.

FREEDOM FROM SELF-CONDEMNATION

"For God did not send his Son into the world to condemn the world."
John 3:17

Kirsten began her treatment with me because she was sabotaging her career and couldn't understand why. She had worked her way to the top of the organization and now spent hours each day unable to perform her work due to a growing panic about being fired. She was almost crippled by feelings of insecurity.

It took several months, but we finally came to some understanding of why she was torpedoing her success. Kirsten was not really proud of herself for her accomplishments. In fact, she wasn't proud of herself at all. Kirsten hated herself and was trying to cover that up with corporate success and material wealth. She was trying to look good on the outside because she believed she was bad on the inside. Kirsten was in the grips of self-condemnation.

Kirsten's childhood was spent cleaning up after her alcoholic mother and trying to hide her embarrassment from the outside world. She lived most of the time either frightened or ashamed. To make matters worse, her mother stopped drinking during Kirsten's adolescence, and since that time has devoted her life to helping others less fortunate than herself. She had made amends to Kirsten and the family, for which Kirsten was supposed to be thankful.

Kirsten thought she hated herself because of how she felt about her mother. It turned out that it wasn't really herself that she hated—it was her mother. Kirsten had never allowed herself to be angry with her mother for the terror and humiliation she went through as a child. Kirsten was supposed to cope with problems and make things look good. But the truth was, she had always blamed herself for her mother's failures. She believed if she had been a better child, her mother wouldn't have had to drink, and she ultimately came to believe that she wasn't worth the effort for her own mother to take care of her. As long as she condemned herself for her miserable childhood, Kirsten was certain she did not deserve to succeed in life.

Once Kirsten began to realize this, however, things changed. When she condemned herself, she lived as though her destiny to fail in life was a fact. She would never succeed, and that was that. But once she became aware of this belief, it changed from "I will never succeed" to "I have always believed that I would never succeed." Something that was an absolute fact now took on the quality of a subjective belief. Facts don't change, but beliefs do.

Kirsten no longer lives as though her failure in life is a predetermined fact. She knows that she has believed this for years, and beliefs can change. She is establishing new beliefs about herself that challenge the old one. She is in the process of forgiving her mother for her childhood, but she had to become aware that she was angry with her first. She has gone from knowing she was a failure to realizing that she only believed this to be true.

Jesus knew that people are saved based upon what they believe. This includes salvation from our own self-condemnation. Kirsten was trying to work her way out of something that had nothing to do with the strength of her efforts, but everything to do with the strength of what she believed. The hard part was finding the beliefs about herself that were the roots of her self-condemnation. Once we did this, her ability to change came much easier.

Everybody feels bad at times about the things they have done, but some people feel bad about who they are. They condemn themselves and become self-destructive unless they discover how to change their beliefs about themselves. Presenting these people with facts rarely changes their attitude of self-condemnation. However, Jesus taught that beliefs are changed by faith, not facts.

Jesus did not come into the world to condemn it. He was not interested in people feeling bad about themselves; rather, Jesus wanted people to feel loved by God. He knew that it is healthy to feel guilty at times, but that self-condemnation results in believing that being bad is an absolute fact that cannot be changed. Self-condemnation is not humility—it's humiliation. Jesus wanted people to find freedom from condemnation, not get stuck in it.

SPIRITUAL PRINCIPLE: Self-condemnation is believing a lie about yourself.

WHY WE JUMP TO CONCLUSIONS

"It is what comes out of a man that makes him 'unclean.'"
Mark 7:15

Jesus taught that human beings are "meaning makers." We *search* for meaning in life, and we automatically *make* meaning out of our circumstances. He said that if anything is "unclean" to someone it is because of the meaning it carries inside that person. He knew that everything we do in life is only as good as the meaning it conveys. Two people can be doing the exact same thing, yet for one it is meaningful and for the other it is not. You can't fully know the appropriateness of a behavior without knowing what is going on in someone's heart.

Without realizing it, we are making interpretations about everything we do based upon our past experiences. This is why we jump to conclusions about things. We are trying to make meaning out of the events of our lives. This can be a problem when we jump to erroneous conclusions about ourselves without realizing we are doing so.

Remember Kirsten? She was having trouble at her job because she thought she hated herself and didn't deserve to succeed. However, the trouble she was having at work just served to confirm her bad feelings about herself. The meaning she made out of her career struggles was that she was an awful person who lacked the character to succeed under stress. Without realizing it, the meaning she was making out of her distress was the very thing that was holding her back. She was turning an emotional issue into a moral one. If she was emotionally distressed, she interpreted that as meaning she was weak. She knew other people who had had a difficult childhood and seemed to be doing fine. She was convinced that she had some character flaw that prevented her from doing better, and each time she struggled she was only further convinced that this was a fact.

Often it isn't what we do that is the issue—it's what we mean by doing it. This is why Jesus said, "All these evils come from inside and make a man 'unclean'" (Mark 7:23). It's a matter of the heart. The fact that we make meaning out of things is both good and bad. It's good when it drives us toward making the world a better place while we are looking for personal meaning in life. It's bad when we jump to conclusions that confirm bad things about ourselves. Having an event mean something bad about us is preferable to no meaning at all. We can't help ourselves. Because of this propensity to keep deriving meaning from circumstances at any cost, it is to our advantage to be humble about what we think we know about ourselves. We could be jumping to negative conclusions without knowing it.

SPIRITUAL PRINCIPLE: Be humble with your conclusion about yourself; it's just your opinion.

BE AS HUMBLE AS ALBERT EINSTEIN

"Whoever humbles himself like this child is the greatest in the
kingdom of heaven."
Matthew 18:4

Heinz Kohut, past president of the American Psychoanalytic Association, thought the future of psychoanalysis depended upon its ability to apply the advancements in the physical sciences to the work being done in therapy.[4] One of these advancements was Albert Einstein's notion that the laws of science are absolute facts, but we observe them relative to our position in space and time. We can only understand things from our own perspective. To say this another way, if you are flying in an airplane and you hand someone a pencil, that pencil is going up to six hundred miles an hour. Yet it does not appear to be going that fast to you. Einstein taught that truth is not relative, but our knowledge of it is.

I apply this in my practice as a psychologist regularly. Recently, I was counseling a couple caught in an ongoing argument over whether or not their one-year-old baby girl should be allowed to sleep in their room at night. After weeks of discussion, Raymond, the father, insisted that the baby should sleep in her own bed, and he was no longer willing to negotiate the matter. Felicia, his wife, was very hurt by this and accused him of being abusive.

"Wait a minute!" Raymond responded. "I've spent months losing sleep and agonizing over the tears of my child every night. Now that we are taking a firm stand, she is able to sleep much more soundly and everyone is happier. My pleas to resolve this matter have fallen upon deaf ears time and time again. I feel as if I'm the one who has been abused here!"

So who was right? It depends upon your perspective. When we insist our perspective is the only valid one in a human exchange, we are going to run into problems. From one perspective,

Raymond seems abusive toward Felicia; from another, he appears loving and protective toward his daughter. The truth of the matter was relative to the perspective of each of the parties.

Both Einstein and Jesus recognized the relationship between knowledge and humility. Einstein told us that understanding is relative to the observer. Jesus told us that whoever humbles himself is the greatest. Woven into the teachings of Jesus two thousand years ago was the notion that we must not consider ourselves to have the absolute say in our relationships with others. Perhaps Jesus was saying spiritually what Einstein would say years later scientifically, that our own perspectives influence each of us as we seek to understand the reality around us. Because of this, true knowledge is humble.

SPIRITUAL PRINCIPLE: True knowledge is humble.

TRUTH IS NOT RELATIVE

"Simply let your 'Yes' be 'Yes,' and your 'No,' 'No.'"
Matthew 5:37

Mrs. Parker called me in a panic. Her son, Nathan, had dropped out of high school and been arrested for drunk driving, and she feared his life was slipping further out of control. After a few minutes of conversation, I invited the entire family in for therapy.

Mr. and Mrs. Parker had only one directive for Nathan, "We just want you to be happy." They thought they were raising him to be objective when they avoided punishing him as a child and offered him alternatives instead. For instance, rather than establishing a set bedtime for him during grade school, they would say, "Nathan, do you want to choose to stay up and be tired all day tomorrow, or do you want to choose to go to bed now and feel rested and alert instead?" Nathan was tired often as a child. The Parkers didn't want to be authoritarian with Nathan, so they tried to teach him that everything is relative, depending upon the choices one makes.

Nathan, however, grew up feeling that his parents didn't know what they were doing. He thought that was why they were always asking him what he should do. Nathan's life was out of control because he had come to feel responsible for controlling it long before he was able to assume that responsibility. When you are seven years old and believe that no one is running the universe, then you come to the conclusion that nothing matters. To Nathan, truth was relative, and reality was what you made of it.

Actually, Nathan needed his parents to know things. As a child, he needed them to set limits, provide security for him, and be straightforward in their answers to his questions. Forcing a child to think for himself too early can have negative consequences. Nathan needed to learn that truth is not relative,[5] even if each of us has our own subjective perspective on it. The Parkers missed the first part of this equation when they were raising their son.

Things are still pretty rough at times for the Parker family, but they are getting better. Mr. and Mrs. Parker have come to admit that they want a few more things for Nathan than they were willing to verbalize before. They want him to be respectful, responsible, and pleasant to be around. They always wanted these things, but they thought imposing their desires on him would damage his happiness. Ironically, as his parents become clearer about what they want from him, Nathan is becoming a happier young man. Respecting each other's point of view does not mean that everything is relative.

Believing that truth is relative and that nothing really matters is exactly the opposite of what Jesus taught. In fact, everything matters. It's just that we have to consider ourselves in a relationship with truth. This is why Jesus said, "I am the Truth" (John 14:6). He knew we don't objectively understand the most profound truths in life—we have relationships with them. We never stop making interpretations about what we perceive. This means we are never truly objective about anything.

Observing the relationship between humility and knowledge does not mean that everybody's ideas are the same or that everything is relative. Neither Jesus nor Einstein was a relativist in this sense. Both believed that absolute truth exists, but we can only know it from our own perspective.

Believing that truth is relative implies that there is no objective truth, so each of us might as well do whatever we like since "everything is relative anyway." Einstein never said this. The speed of light is the speed of light. Jesus certainly was not a relativist. He taught us to let our "Yes be Yes" because he wanted us to be people of conviction. Reality isn't relative; there are absolutes. But we can only know these absolutes from our own perspective.

SPIRITUAL PRINCIPLE: Believe in the truth with conviction; approach it with humility.

HUMILITY IS NOT PASSIVITY

*"If someone strikes you on the right cheek, turn to him the
other also."*
Matthew 5:39

We often speak of passive people as being humble. It is a way of
finding something nice to say about people we secretly think are
rather ineffective. Especially in American culture, we rarely
admire humility because we perceive it to be the opposite of
aggressiveness, which we associate with success.

But Jesus had a different view of humility. He said, "Now that
I, your Lord and Teacher, have washed your feet, you also should
wash one another's feet" (John 13:14). Jesus did not humble
himself in the presence of others because he had low self-esteem.
He chose to serve them because he knew who he was; he was
confident enough to take the servant role. He knew important
status doesn't make a man great, but a great man will always be
important to others.

Humility requires confidence. Humility is knowing who you
are and choosing to serve others. It is not self-effacement out of
insecurity. Being able to make someone else feel important without feeling diminished yourself is true humility.

One of my joys as a child was playing dominoes with my
grandfather. This was a very serious game for him. He was raised
in a small town in Arkansas where skill at this game could establish a man's reputation for miles. Where he came from, people
took dominoes seriously.

As he was teaching me the game, I came to realize that it was
a tremendous disadvantage to not be able to see your opponent's
game pieces. If I played the wrong piece, he could score off of my
move and I might lose the game. As ten-year-old boys sometimes
do, one day I acted impulsively on my idea about how to solve
this problem. I reached over and began knocking down all of his

game pieces so I could see whether or not my next move was going to be a good one.

Instinctively, he raised himself up from his chair in horror at what I was doing. Almost gasping, he tensed up, then caught himself in midair. Just as quickly as he had jerked himself from his seat, he reversed himself and slowly sat back down with a somewhat knowing smile emerging on his face. Although I had observed this strange behavior, I didn't understand its meaning until much later.

Even though he had struggled to get where he was in life, my grandfather knew that winning wasn't everything. To him, the object of the game in life wasn't to get the most points; it was to play so as to get the most respect from your opponent. I remember that dominoes game with my grandfather because it came to symbolize our relationship. It wasn't how good he looked that was important to him; it was how good he could make me look instead.

I didn't get away with knocking those game pieces down that day because my grandfather was too passive to stop me. It was because he was teaching me something about humility. Humility is strength under control. It took many such events in my life before I saw this, but my grandfather taught me about humility in a very powerful way—he modeled it for me.

Passivity is refusing to make a statement out of fear. Humility is making a statement out of love. This is what Jesus meant when he said, "If someone strikes you on the right cheek, turn to him the other also." He didn't say, "If someone strikes you on the cheek, turn and walk away." He specifically instructed people to take a stand and make a statement. The point he was trying to make with others is that love is stronger than hatred. If people attack you out of hatred, love them to death. Jesus lived this out in his own life quite literally. He preferred a shorter life filled with humility and love over a longer life filled with passivity and fear.

SPIRITUAL PRINCIPLE: Humility is strength under control.

WHY THERAPISTS MUST BE HUMBLE

"Blessed are the poor in spirit, for theirs is the kingdom of heaven."
Matthew 5:3

Elaine was a shy woman who came for psychotherapy as a result of continual failed relationships. As time went on, it became more and more difficult for us to end our sessions on time. It seemed as though something important would come up in the last few minutes of almost every session, and Elaine would erupt into painful feelings and tears that made the conclusion of our sessions difficult for both of us.

At first I thought that our forty-five minute sessions were just not long enough for her. It seemed as though she had a well of emotion inside that would erupt like a geyser as a result of our conversations. But this perspective on Elaine was portraying her as "too emotional" to end on time, and I rarely view people as "too emotional" because that only reinforces a negative view of people for having their feelings.

Then it occurred to me. That earlier perspective left *me* completely out of the formulation. Near the end of each session I found myself trying to bring the conversation to a close. I did not want to get into anything too deep if we only had a few minutes left. Without realizing it, I was subtly cutting Elaine off. To me, I was trying to help Elaine out by avoiding uncovering anything we did not have the time to get into. To Elaine, I was rejecting her and telling her I didn't want to hear about how she felt anymore.

Because I couldn't listen to her anymore due to time constraints, she felt as if I didn't want to. It was the meaning of the ending of the sessions that was painful for Elaine, not that she was overflowing with emotions too overwhelming for her to control. Once we both came to this realization, the endings of our sessions together started to go much smoother. It still hurt to end, but it eventually stopped feeling like rejection. The difficulty that was in need of treatment was not something defective inside of Elaine; it was something in our relationship that was in need of attention.

Jesus taught that the "poor in spirit" will inherit treasures because of their humility. Therapists must be humble in order to inherit the treasures that lie in their relationships with their patients. Many therapists believe that the relationship established in therapy is what helps people.[6] Psychologists must listen very carefully to each patient as they discover together how this new relationship they are forming can be healing. They are applying in their consultation rooms what Jesus said to be true about inheriting the Kingdom of God.

This may sound as if these therapists don't know much, that all they do is sit around and listen to their patients without any idea of where they are going or what they should be doing. Nothing could be further from the truth. In fact, they must be even more skillful, for therapists must be analyzing themselves along with their patients.

To Jesus, a healer always thinks of himself or herself as in relationship with others. People don't simply come for healing; they enter into a relationship with the one offering the healing.

SPIRITUAL PRINCIPLE: Therapy is more than a process; it's a relationship.

JESUS THE THERAPIST

"Love each other."
John 15:17

When Sheila came for her first session with me, she announced that I was her seventh therapist since college, so she knew both her diagnosis and the theoretical orientation with which I was to treat her. "I have a borderline personality disorder. Of course, you know there is no cure," she reported.

Nothing strikes more fear in the heart of a therapist than the term "borderline," so she had my complete attention.

"And how is it that you have come to this conclusion?" I asked.

"My last therapist made it very clear to me. You better look it up, because I need someone who knows what they are doing," she said with an antagonistic tone.

It quickly became apparent that her previous therapist had labeled her as "borderline" because of her intense and unstable relationships, flashes of rage, and suffocating fear of abandonment. She did qualify for this diagnosis, which is a difficult disorder to treat in light of the anger and abuse that therapists suffer in the process.

As time went on it was apparent that Sheila anticipated rejection from me, so she was constantly engaging in desperate acts to get me to take her seriously and commit myself to her treatment. Suicidal threats, emergency phone calls at three o'clock in the morning, sexual liaisons with strangers, and violent outbursts in my office were all designed to intensify our relationship, because she lived with the constant threat of its ending at any moment.

I came to see that diagnosing Sheila with a "borderline personality disorder" had become part of the problem. If we were both anticipating Sheila to act in an outrageous manner because of some inherent defect in her, that is what we would see. Sheila wasn't suffering from an innate pathological rage that forced her to be destructive; she was a person who was desperately trying to rescue herself as well as her endangered relationship with me. She wasn't trying to be destructive any more than a drowning person is trying to kill the rescuer who swims up too close. The experienced lifeguard knows that people who believe they are dying will do anything to save themselves, including taking the lifeguard down with them. Desperate people do desperate things to save themselves.

As soon as I stopped seeing Sheila as fighting *with* me and started seeing her as fighting *for* herself in our relationship, our power struggles began to decline. Focusing on her accurate diagnosis became less important as understanding her desperate attempts to relate to me came more into focus.

Sheila is still a difficult person to be around sometimes, but the dramatic behavior that was so common a few years ago has decreased. Having a diagnosis is less important to her now because feeling genuinely connected to me, and others, has made it so. She still has an edge about her, but she is more loving than before, because she has a better sense of what it feels like to be loved herself.

We now have the psychological theories to help us understand the ancient teachings of Jesus in a more profound way than before. Jesus taught that instead of relying upon dogma, we should rely upon a loving relationship with God. Relationship was the key, not being right about things. This is what many therapists believe today.

Jesus said, "This is my command: Love each other." Love is the glue that binds relationships together. It is the substance that makes humans form indivisible units with each other. Love is the spiritual term for the genuine connection many therapists endeavor to establish with their patients.

Many therapists are saying we need to take the emphasis off of technical diagnoses and theories and place it upon the relationship established in therapy. Jesus was saying we need to take the emphasis off of legalistic approaches to religion and technical definitions of righteousness and place it upon our relationships with God and others. Whether it's psychological health or spiritual salvation, taking the emphasis off of our objective knowledge and placing it upon our relational experience is the key. This humble approach to knowledge in the teachings of Jesus can be found in the consultation rooms of many therapists today.

SPIRITUAL PRINCIPLE: Never let your dogma become your master.

Pleasant Street
United Methodist Church
Waterville, ME 04901

CHAPTER 2

UNDERSTANDING PEOPLE:
ARE THEY GOOD OR BAD?

Jesus said: "A man was going down from Jerusalem to Jericho,
when he fell into the hands of robbers. They stripped him of his
clothes, beat him and went away, leaving him half dead. A
priest happened to be going down the same road, and when he
saw the man, he passed by on the other side. So too, a Levite,
when he came to the place and saw him, passed by on the other
side. But a Samaritan, as he traveled, came where the man
was; and when he saw him, he took pity on him. He went to
him and bandaged his wounds, pouring on oil and wine.
Then he put the man on his own donkey, took him to an inn
and took care of him. The next day he took out two silver coins
and gave them to the innkeeper. 'Look after him,' he said, 'and
when I return, I will reimburse you for any extra expense you
may have.'"

Luke 10:30–35

Are people basically good or bad? Eventually, most of us come to one
of these two conclusions about human nature. But if we look at how
Jesus spoke about people psychologically, it appears as though he
hadn't come to either conclusion.

Some of us are like the priest and Levite in the parable, others like
the Samaritan, others like the robbers, and still others like the man who
was beaten and left for dead. But what made the Samaritan act the
way he did? Was it because he was basically a good person? Jesus
repeatedly tried to make the point that the most basic aspect of human
nature is our need for a relationship with God and others. From this
perspective, people aren't basically either good or bad. What they are
is relational. Our basic nature is to need relationships. The Samaritan

33

was "good" because he didn't ignore the beaten man and stopped to enter into a relationship with him.

Psychologically, viewing people as simply good or bad is too simplistic. We are tempted to think this way because it is easier than doing the hard work of figuring out our relationships with others. We want to believe we can identify people as either good or bad because we will then know whom to trust and whom to avoid. But the truth is, there are always potential "Samaritans" as well as "robbers" among us. People who recognize their basic need for relationships with others tend to have behavior that is good. They need others, so they don't want to hurt them. The people who violate our basic nature to live in relationship with others turn out to be the bad ones among us.[1]

The parable of the good Samaritan is about good and bad people. Jesus explains the difference between the two in terms of our relationships with others, not our essential goodness or badness. He understood human nature with profound psychological insight and, as a result, can help us today to understand the behavior of everyone we know, even ourselves.

DID JESUS SEE PEOPLE AS BASICALLY BAD?

"A man was going down from Jerusalem to Jericho, when he
fell into the hands of robbers."
Luke 10:30

As a biblical scholar, Jesus was familiar with the Jewish scriptures that taught of God's disappointment with the human race and his eventual destruction of the planet with a great flood.[2] If he concluded from this that we are basically bad, then our nature is to be like the robbers in the good Samaritan parable. We will take what we can from others because this world is about the survival of the fittest and it is our nature to look out for ourselves first. In this view, without some form of religion or restraint, we would all turn out to be hurtful and destructive.

Martin is a very intelligent and highly educated man. He has successfully built two businesses from the ground up and then completely bankrupted both of them. Martin is articulate, persuasive, and often gets what he wants. The problem is that Martin never wants what he gets.

Martin came for therapy briefly because his wife insisted that they get professional help or she was going to divorce him. She had discovered that he was having an affair with another woman and that his drug problem was much more serious than he had led her to believe. Martin was frequently dishonest with his wife, and she was coming to the realization that she didn't even know the man she had married. He was involved in a number of illegal activities he had kept secret from his wife, and he didn't want a messy divorce to expose him. Martin felt anxious at times about getting caught for his misdeeds, but he never felt guilty about them. As far as I could tell, Martin seemed to be a genuinely bad person, even if he didn't think so.

Martin is the robber in the parable of the good Samaritan. He steals from others and then squanders his booty, leading him to steal again. There *are* bad people in life who violate others and leave them depleted and abused. The tragedy is that each time Martin abuses someone, he hurts himself. This only makes him want to take advantage of someone else again. His lack of compassion for others has created a wall around his heart that cuts him off from his own humanity. Without access to his own human compassion, he becomes less able to respond in a good way to others. Martin is caught up in an addicting cycle of abuse toward others. Ironically, it is because he has lost touch with any feelings of being bad that he continues to act badly toward others.

Jesus doesn't mention any confrontation of the robbers in the parable of the good Samaritan, because confronting robbers with their immorality does little good. They usually tell you what you want to hear anyway. Some people like Martin can change, but only under extreme circumstances. I don't know what might have happened if Martin had stayed in therapy long enough and I had been able to develop a significant enough relationship with him to get him to take an honest look at himself. As it was, he continued to act badly toward people because no one was important enough to him to get him to act otherwise. Martin's wife did divorce him, and I don't know where he is today, but it's probably no place good.

In the parable of the good Samaritan, the robbers were definitely bad people, but Jesus placed his focus elsewhere. He wasn't interested in exposing human nature as bad; he was interested in providing us with a model for how to be good. Jesus was constantly associating with people who might have been considered "bad" by others—tax collectors, sinners—but he didn't view them that way himself. He saw all people as capable of being good and never treated them as if they were anything other than that. He was constantly inviting people into a relationship with him because that was what gave them the power to be good.

SPIRITUAL PRINCIPLE: To steal from others robs the thief of a soul.

THE PROBLEM WITH THE VIEW OF PEOPLE AS BAD

*"On the outside you appear to people as righteous but on the
inside you are full of hypocrisy and wickedness."*
Matthew 23:28

Joshua came for therapy because his marriage was falling apart.
He was referred to me by his marriage therapist, who thought he
could benefit from individual therapy. Joshua was a devoutly religious man who was always interested in doing the right thing
whenever he could. If going to individual therapy would help his
marriage, then he was certainly willing to go.

The problem Joshua and I encountered early on in his therapy
was that he believed his real problem was his wife. It was difficult
for Joshua to discuss anything other than how she had disappointed him, failed to live up to her part of the marriage vows,
and was destroying their marriage through her self-centeredness.
Joshua would give a cursory look at his contributions to the marriage problems, but he consistently ended his self-evaluation with
statements like, "But I feel fine. If it weren't for her, I wouldn't
even be here."

Joshua viewed himself as a spiritual person who had invested
years educating himself theologically, cultivating his faith as well
as giving time to support the spiritual growth of others. He was
firmly convinced that if people practiced the spiritual disciplines,
they wouldn't have emotional problems. He was certain his
wife's problems stemmed from a lack of faith.

Joshua couldn't understand his wife's psychological problems
or his own contributions to his marital difficulties. He believed
that giving over to human emotions was submitting to "the
flesh," which he believed to be basically bad. Joshua wanted to be
a spiritual person who was able to rise above his human weak-
nesses. He was critical of his wife for failing to do the same.

I tried to get Joshua to see that expressing emotions was not a sign of weakness, but, rather, evidence of strength. But Joshua's conviction that humanity was basically corrupt would not allow him to entertain this notion. "My faith is based upon facts, not feelings," he informed me. To place facts and feelings on equal footing was a violation of his faith. As a result, he couldn't value his wife's feelings as important contributions to their lives, and he continued to see them as deviant expressions of a fallen humanity that needed to be disavowed.

Unfortunately, my therapy with Joshua was brief and unsuccessful. I always find it difficult to help people who come for therapy because they believe someone other than themselves really needs the help. Yet a greater barrier to Joshua's success in therapy was his belief that humanity is basically bad and spiritual people should try to divorce themselves from it. We were fundamentally at odds. I was trying to get him to get in touch with his humanity, and he was trying to get as far away from it as possible.

The problem with believing that people are basically bad is that it makes you feel ashamed for being human. You then create a persona through which you can pretend to be something other than what you are. Because humanity is wretched and bad, you must find a way to be set free from the bad part and become a spiritual being living above it all. The problem the Pharisees fell into was believing that they weren't like everyone else. They thought they were more spiritual and less human.

In other words, believing that people are basically bad can produce "superspirituality." Those who believe that humanity is morally defective want to distance themselves from it as much as possible. They only want to associate with those who hold identical religious beliefs. They invest time and energy in creating a persona that is identifiably distinct from people they would consider to be "of the world." And they develop disdain, even if it is unconscious, for those who fail to achieve their level of spirituality. Once they have achieved a higher level of existence, they defend themselves from any indication of falling back into a more common level of humanity. In psychological terms, this persona is called a false self. The religious term is a Pharisee.

When Jesus told the parable of the good Samaritan, there was intense racial prejudice between Jews and Samaritans. Back then, Samaritans were considered bad people, and Pharisees, the priests and devoutly religious people among the Jews, were considered good. The fact that Jesus himself was a Jew made the moral of the story all the more powerful. Today the terms are reversed. "Good" and "Samaritan" go automatically together in our speech, and to be called a "Pharisee" is certainly a bad thing.

Jesus was making a keen psychological observation in this parable. Holding prejudices against people hurts us more than them. People are good or bad based upon the relationships they have, not because of something inherent in them from birth. We cannot rise above our humanity with our religion—we live it to its fullest because of it.

SPIRITUAL PRINCIPLE: You can't escape your self—but you can find it.

ARE PEOPLE BASICALLY GOOD?

"But a Samaritan . . . took pity on him."
Luke 10:33

I lean toward believing in the inherent goodness of people because of those like Lorraine. She came for therapy shortly following the death of her mother. She had some negative feelings toward her mother that made grieving her death more difficult.

Although Lorraine began treatment looking for support to help her through a difficult time, she discovered that there were many things about herself that she needed to understand better. Lorraine had a difficult childhood with an alcoholic mother that resulted in a tendency to deny her own needs in her relationships with others. To make matters worse, she seemed to have an uncanny ability to select men who looked fine on the outside but were psychologically dysfunctional and emotionally unavailable.

Fortunately, Lorraine had a genuine desire to grow. As painful as it was, she rarely missed her sessions because she was intent upon knowing herself better and getting free from the pattern of dysfunctional choices she had made in the past. I looked forward to my sessions with Lorraine because she seemed to benefit from our work together so naturally. Something within her motivated her to keep trying to change what she could to make her life better.

Lorraine has grown a lot over the past several years. She used to be shy, somewhat of a workaholic, and constantly trying to get out of some relationship with an abusive man. Today she has changed to a profession that allows her to control her future better, has become a respected leader in her community, and is dating men who are more her equal. Lorraine is a good person. In spite of the difficulties she has had in life, the people who know her can feel it.

If people are not basically bad, then perhaps they are inherently good, a view of human nature many therapists find attractive. Jesus certainly seemed to love people of all ages, races, and socioeconomic levels. His love for others was unconditional, which communicated his belief in the intrinsic worth of each person he met.

Perhaps our nature is to be like the good Samaritan. If we could set aside all the influences of busy schedules and demanding pressures, we might find a fundamental altruism within each of us. If we look closely enough, we could find something to love in even the most difficult people. What if our nature was to be basically good if only we could get past the defenses and past hurts that keep us from displaying it?

As attractive as this way of viewing people might be, this isn't exactly what Jesus believed about human nature either. There is a difference between intrinsic worth and inherent goodness. The point of the good Samaritan parable is that we are not all good people. We need to look closely at the teachings of Jesus to determine why.

SPIRITUAL PRINCIPLE: "Infants don't sin." *The Talmud*

DID JESUS SEE PEOPLE AS BASICALLY GOOD?

"Love your enemies."
Luke 6:27

The philosophy that asserts that people are basically good is called humanism. Because of Jesus' love for others and his concern for the welfare of everyone he met, he is often held up as one of the great examples of the ideal humanist. Jesus taught that we should love everyone, even our enemies. It is certainly easy to see how Jesus could be used as an example of someone who believed in the basic goodness of people.

Carl Rogers is one of the best-known psychologists to develop a theory based upon the belief in the essential goodness of humanity.[3] He believed all people have within them a "self-actualizing process" that will drive them toward health under the right conditions. Rogerian therapy, named after Dr. Rogers, is familiar to almost every therapist as one of the primary examples of humanistic psychology.

What many people don't know is that Dr. Rogers experienced a religious conversion to Christianity while he was at the University of Wisconsin and then went to Union Theological Seminary to pursue religious studies. However, he became disillusioned with the academic study of theology and switched to child guidance and psychology.

One day, while talking with the mother of a difficult child he was attempting to treat in psychotherapy, Dr. Rogers came to an important realization. After he had finished his discussion of the child's problems, the mother got up and began to leave the room. Just as she got to the door she hesitated, then turned to Dr. Rogers, and said, "You know, we have a few minutes left. Do you mind if I bring up a few things about myself?" Rogers set aside his complicated psychological theories for a moment and actively listened to the woman. In his own words, "Real therapy began." He went on to discover what he believed to be an innate drive toward wholeness within each person that becomes activated in the presence of what he called the unconditional positive regard of another human being. I don't know if Dr. Rogers ever credits Jesus with inspiring him to come up with his theory, but there are some striking similarities in his thinking to the unconditional love that Jesus taught centuries ago.

Jesus spoke of divine love, which was unconditional. Rogers spoke of unconditional positive regard as essential to the healing process. Jesus described humanity as being in the image of God, having inherent worth. Rogers observed an organismic self-actualizing process inherent in all people. Jesus said he embodied the truth within his person. Rogers said authenticity comes only from being congruent with one's self.

Jesus had a lot to say that supports the humanistic belief in the inherent goodness of people, but we cannot stop here and do him justice. Jesus also acknowledged the problems associated with such a belief. For that we will have to read on . . .

SPIRITUAL PRINCIPLE: Good listeners make good people.

THE PROBLEM WITH THE VIEW OF PEOPLE AS GOOD

"So the last will be first, and the first will be last."
Matthew 20:16

Tyler is a promising young executive with a bright future in business. He is sharp, good-looking, and ambitious. Tyler likes to think of himself as self-actualized because he is independent and good at everything he does. His definition of strength is self-reliance under even the most extreme conditions.

Tyler came for therapy with his girlfriend because she thought they could benefit from some relationship counseling. He didn't think he needed it personally, but he was always open to learning how to be more effective in life. "We're just here for a tune-up," he advised me. "I'm not interested in a long drawn-out process of discussing my feelings about my mother or anything." Tyler didn't like to look back because he saw himself as always moving forward, and discussing the past seemed like a contradiction to him.

Tyler's view of their relationship was that it was an attempt to form a partnership. He was interested in a merger of potentials. He was willing to invest in the relationship, but only if he would get an acceptable return on his investment. He didn't want someone who was dependent upon him; he wanted a partner who was going to make an equal contribution.

"Traditional roles may have worked in previous generations, but unless you're willing to spend some time as a D.I.N.K., you're never going to get ahead these days. We are two progressive individuals, and that's what works about us," Tyler insisted.

I knew that Double Income No Kids couples were able to live above the financial means of single-income families, but I wondered if financial achievement was going to be enough to satisfy Tyler in the long run.

"So, do you think children might be something you two might want in the future?" I asked.

"Maybe someday," Tyler responded. "But we're enjoying our freedom too much right now."

Tyler's highest value was independence. He was trying to figure out how to couple with someone without sacrificing anything of himself in the process. He was only interested in marriage if he could think of it as a joint effort by two individuals, like an experimental partnership that could be dissolved if it didn't turn out to provide him with the promised benefit.

Although Tyler could never admit it, he was actually basing his relationships upon the traditional ones he found so inadequate. Tyler wanted to have a relationship that was exactly the opposite of the one his parents had. Ironically, this means his parents' relationship was the defining model for his own. As much as he hated to look into the past, that is exactly where he needed to look if he was going to understand his future.

Over the course of our counseling Tyler came to see that his desire to be an "individual" meant that he was disappointed with how others had done things, and he wanted to do his life differently. He began to recognize that he was not free from his past at all. Rather than being independent, Tyler came to realize that he was actually dependent upon his past and other people, to the extent that he was trying to avoid them without being aware he was doing so.

Tyler's relationship with his girlfriend is going pretty well now. They communicate better about their feelings, and their expectations for their relationship have changed. They still have rather ambitious financial goals, but they are discussing them as just one of a set of goals for their relationship. Tyler is starting to depend upon someone emotionally, and he is finding that his dependence is producing greater dividends than he had imagined before. Instead of "looking out for number one," he is starting to "become one" with his girlfriend, and he is finding that more satisfying.

Individualism is the belief in self-reliance and personal independence. It is based upon the belief that all people are essentially good and stresses personal achievement and success without having to depend upon others. All you really need is yourself.

For those who believe in individualism, the modern substitute for salvation has become *personal* psychological health. If anything impinges upon their personal rights, they get rid of it. They feel entitled to achieve their personal best at any cost.

I refer to this as the "myth" of individualism because human beings don't really work that way. To feel like an individual, one needs a group from which to feel distinct. The experience of individualism actually requires a relationship with others. We human beings have a fundamental need for others in order to know who we are. Just as we need mirrors to reflect our physical images, to give us the sense of how we look physically, we need other people to bounce off of emotionally, to give us the sense of who we are psychologically.

Jesus' idea that "the first will be last" is the opposite of individualism. Although he recognized the inherent worth of each person, people were only good as a result of their relationships with God and others. Jesus never thought we could be good all by ourselves. To him, we do not achieve our best through competition, but through connection.

SPIRITUAL PRINCIPLE: The individual is a part of the whole.

PEOPLE ARE NEITHER GOOD NOR BAD

"I have called you friends."
John 15:15

Jesus was illustrating a point about human nature in the parable of the good Samaritan. He wasn't saying we are fundamentally bad like the robbers or automatically good like the Samaritan. Our essential nature, according to Jesus, is relational. Our basic need is for relationships with each other in order to be whole.

The Samaritan will be remembered throughout history as "good" because of his relationship with the beaten man. The Levite and the priest weren't bad; they were just too busy. We often use the excuse that we are too busy in order to insulate ourselves from the realization that we are vitally connected to others. They need us, and even more frightening to accept is the fact that we need them.

The most difficult area in my life in which to accept the notion that I am a fundamentally relational being has been in my relationship with my father. We seldom saw things eye to eye and argued often, and I can remember only a few times in my life when I did not feel tense around him. Our relationship was strained right up until his death.

I remember receiving the news that my father had been diagnosed with cancer. I was in shock, partly because I think I was living with the illusion that these things happened to other people and partly because I was not ready for him to die. I knew our relationship was not good, and I didn't want him to leave my life until we could do something about it.

Although we hadn't communicated with each other much since I became an adult, I made plans to fly back to Tulsa to spend the weekend with him once the doctors had sent him home from the hospital. They said they couldn't do anything more for him there.

I didn't know what I was going to say, but I wanted to have some sort of conversation with him that didn't end up with one of us getting angry. It was going to be one of the most important moments of my life.

I'll never forget my last evening with him. I was sitting on the edge of his bed, groping for the words to express my regret over our painful relationship. Quite uncharacteristically he said to me, "Mark, you know we haven't talked much since you left home. Why don't you tell me about your life now?"

Without thinking I blurted out, "It's never been easy for us to talk."

He calmly replied, "Well, if we bowed our heads, would you pray that we could have a conversation right now? You do that so well."

In tears, I did just that. For the next four hours I had the best conversation with my father I had ever had in my life. Actually, I think it was the only real one. I found out things about his life I never knew, and I told him things about myself. I asked him to forgive me for leaving home so angrily years ago, and I will live the rest of my life with the knowledge that the last words I ever spoke to my father were "I love you."

One of the lessons I learned that day was that I needed to heal my relationship with my father as much as he needed to repair his relationship with me. He went into a coma the day I left Tulsa and never revived. He had finished his business and was ready to go. What I realized was that I had unfinished business too. In some ways, I was stuck and couldn't go on with my life fully until I repaired my relationship with him. I needed to forgive him, for me.

Who we are is profoundly influenced by our relationships with others. We need them so that we can be healthy ourselves. Just because we are angry with someone doesn't mean we don't have a relationship with him or her. Putting half a continent between my father and me didn't lessen the impact of my relationship with him a bit. My life is better because I had the opportunity to make peace with my father before he died. This has helped me recognize the importance of all my relationships, even the painful ones, in making me who I am.

Looking back on it now, I can see that there was no "bad guy" in my relationship with my father. We were both contributing to the problems we were having and both responsible for doing something about it. There was nothing that was making us fight with each other, and there was only our woundedness that stood in the way of making peace with each other. Just as in the parable of the good Samaritan, we were both living our lives as the beaten man when we felt wounded by the other, the robbers when we perpetuated the hurt between us, and the Levites and the priests when we were too busy to take the time to make things better. Thankfully, we both were trying to be the good Samaritan in the end by stopping to enter into a relationship with each other just before my father died.

Jesus taught that beyond loving others, we should treat those closest to us as friends. This is often a more difficult task than loving them. Although Jesus saw himself as a leader, a prophet, and even the Son of God, when he said to his followers, "I have called you friends," he was making a statement about the essence of people. There is nothing more important than our choice to enter into relationships with those around us, no matter how hard this might be. This is a principle I use in the therapy I practice, and one that has helped me in my personal life as well.

SPIRITUAL PRINCIPLE: Sometimes we treat those we love in ways we would never treat our friends. For this we should ask for forgiveness.

THE IMAGE OF GOD ON EARTH

"The Father is in me, and I in the Father."
John 10:38

Darren is an experienced consumer of psychotherapy. He started going to therapy when he was in high school and has continued seeing therapists off and on for years. Although Darren has been helped by much of the therapy he has received, he has also been under the influence of what I would consider to be outdated forms of treatment.

Darren was very shy and withdrawn. He suffered from a poor self-image and believed that no one was really interested in him. He had few friends and could only socialize in bars after he lowered his inhibitions with significant amounts of alcohol. This, of course, created other problems.

At one point Darren came across a form of therapy that was very liberating for him. He was instructed to go into a room full of other patients and act out whatever emotions he wanted to express. Taking his cue from the others, Darren soon found himself screaming at the top of his lungs and throwing himself on the floor. Suddenly, he was able to express a violent rage that he had kept under control his entire life. Contrary to his expectations, Darren was not rejected for having such angry feelings—he was actually praised for being able to express them so freely. This was liberating. Darren could hardly believe that he could show others the most unacceptable, loathsome parts of himself and still be accepted. To have the deepest parts of ourselves accepted when we fear rejection is very healing.

However, Darren's healing experience didn't last. On some level Darren couldn't believe that the others were genuinely accepting him. He thought that they were only pretending to do so like everyone else he had known. Unconsciously, he wanted to find out if there was still something about him that they wouldn't accept. So his angry outbursts began to escalate. He would not only yell like the others; he would turn over furniture and angrily defy the therapists when they tried to set limits on his behavior.

"But I'm just expressing my true feelings," he would shriek.

"Well, you can't do that here," they finally yelled back.

Darren was eventually asked to leave the therapy group, which hurt him a great deal. His therapists recognized Darren's need to express himself, but they failed to recognize the importance of their relationships with him as he was doing so.

Merely expressing emotions is not healing. Expressing them within the context of a relationship, however, can be. As long as Darren experienced the expression of his feelings as something that made him feel accepted by others, his therapy was healing past wounds for him. Once he felt rejected for his expressions of anger, his therapy became a repetition of past traumas. Psychologists are now recognizing that we are fundamentally relational beings, and our therapy must always be attuned to that.

Jesus taught that we could not live without a relationship with God any more than we could live without air. That relationship was the atmosphere in which humans live. Without it we could not survive. To try to live isolated lives would be to violate our very nature. To recognize our fundamental dependence upon someone outside of ourselves was the only way to fulfill our nature.

Many psychologists are coming to the same conclusion. We are recognizing that people can only have a "self" as they relate to others.[4] The focus on differentiating from others is falling out of favor and is being replaced with the notion that people never stop needing others in order to be healthy.

Jesus adhered to the Jewish creation story that humankind was made in the image of God.[5] But Jesus taught that in the beginning there was God the Father, the Holy Spirit, and the Son (John 1:1). This meant that God had three manifestations, all of which were in relationship with each other. In short, God was a relational being. Thus, our capacity for relationship reflects the image of God on earth.

Jesus always thought of himself as in constant relationship with God. He said, "The Father is in me, and I in the Father." Although he was separate from God, he was still united with him at the same time. This profound connection between them was a model for how he wanted us to think about ourselves. Humans cannot exist in isolation.

SPIRITUAL PRINCIPLE: The image of God in us is our capacity for relationships.

MISUNDERSTANDING THE POINT OF JESUS' LIFE

At first his disciples did not understand . . .
John 12:16

Palm Sunday is remembered in the Christian church as the beginning of the most important week in Jesus' life. It was on this Sunday that Jesus rode into Jerusalem to live out his final days on earth. People who had heard about his coming lined the streets to greet him, waving palm leaves as a symbol of victory for a powerful ruler, much like our ticker-tape parades for war heroes in this country.

Ironically, Jesus came riding in on a donkey. Instead of coming into town in an ostentatious manner, he came on a humble means of transportation to fulfill an ancient prophecy. He wanted to make a point: he wanted people to know he was someone they could relate to. Even Jesus' closest friend, John, later wrote of this event that he "did not understand." People then, and now, tend to assume that if Jesus had the power to change the world, then it should have been obvious to him how disgusting humanity was and he must have had some drastic plans to wipe out the corruption and evil that pervaded the planet. Jesus, on the other hand, seemed to keep telling people that they needed a relationship with God.

My friend Steve isn't interested in religion, especially Christianity. To him, Jesus was some moralistic rabbi who went around acting "holier than thou" and trying to get people to feel guilty if they didn't do the same. Steve believes that religion just brings out the worst in people and preys on their bad feelings about themselves.

Unfortunately, I think a lot of religious people also think as Steve does. Many religious people are religious because they feel guilty and they are hoping that by being religious they can do something to feel better about themselves. They follow religious rituals, give money away, and try to live religious lives so they don't have to feel bad about themselves. The idea that Jesus wanted to point out to people how bad they are and try to get them to live more moral lives misses the point.

Jesus was critical of some people's behavior, but the people he criticized most were religious people. He was rarely judgmental toward average people, and if he did come across someone acting badly, he would tell them to "go and sin no more" without making their bad behavior the focal point of his sermon. The point of Jesus' life was not to focus on how bad people were; it was to let them know that they needed a relationship with God. He believed that if we recognized this basic human need within ourselves, we wouldn't want to act badly. It is easy to misunderstand the point of Jesus' life if we try to make his mission a moral one, if we believe that Jesus saw people as basically wretched and in need of moral deliverance through religious principles and philosophy. The point of Jesus' life wasn't to make us more moral—it was to make us more relational. It seemed to him that good morality would flow out of good relationships, and it doesn't always work the other way around.

SPIRITUAL PRINCIPLE: Good morality flows from good relationships.

GETTING BACK TO THE GARDEN OF EDEN

"I have come that they may have life, and have it to the full."
John 10:10

Michael hasn't spoken to his brother, Tom, in years. Everyone in the family is aware of the antipathy between Michael and Tom, and no one knows what to do about it. Both men are somewhat stubborn, and each feels he has been offended deeply by the other. The last time Michael's wife tried to discuss the situation with him, the conversation ended with Michael yelling, "I don't want his name ever mentioned in this house again."

Actually, neither Michael nor Tom can remember how their feud got started. Yet both of them can remember numerous incidents they use to keep the hate between them going. Michael is furious with Tom for not being the kind of older brother he needed, and Tom is equally furious with Michael for being so resentful of him. Each feels entitled to amends from the other, and neither is interested in doing anything about it.

What neither Michael nor Tom realizes is that they both need each other to be whole. The war between them results in mutually wounded souls. In spite of what Freud originally thought, it is not natural for family members to be aggressive toward each other. This kind of antipathy is a sign of something wrong.

Michael is in need of reconciliation with Tom for his own sake. He resists approaching his brother to repair the rift between them because he thinks it would be "giving in" to him. The irony is that Michael is withholding something from himself by allowing the falling out to continue. Reconciling broken relationships heals the wounds in our own souls. There is a bitterness and anger in Michael that affects all of his relationships because of the broken relationship he has with Tom. Being right has little to do with improving the quality of Michael's life. Reconciling to his brother does.

Jesus saw his life's work as the reconciliation of humankind to God. The Jewish Scriptures taught that Adam and Eve had been exiled from the Garden of Eden because of their disobedience to God. Theologically, this event has been called the Fall, because humanity had fallen from favor with God. The mission of Jesus was to show us the way home.

When I think about the Fall from the perspective of a psychologist, I ask the question, "Fallen from what?" The answer that Jesus would give is, "Fallen from a relationship with God." What humankind lost in the Garden of Eden was our intimate relationship with God. Jesus saw himself as the bridge between God and us. This was our redemption, restored relationship to God.

I believe our lives would go better if we thought about our own redemption in terms of restored relationships more often. Most people think in terms of finding out who is at fault when a relationship has been broken. When we get hurt, we want to make it a moral issue. If we feel bad, then a bad person must have done this to us. Then the only way to make things right is for someone to pay. Jesus, on the other hand, thought things could be made right by what we *give* to others, not by what we *get* from them in the way of payment.

SPIRITUAL PRINCIPLE: Redemption is restored relationships.

CHAPTER 3

UNDERSTANDING GROWTH

"No one sews a patch of unshrunk cloth on an old garment, for the patch will pull away from the garment, making the tear worse. Neither do men pour new wine into old wineskins. If they do, the skins will burst, the wine will run out and the wineskins will be ruined. No, they pour new wine into new wineskins, and both are preserved."

Matthew 9:16–17

Jesus taught that people who are growing are always prepared to change their thinking about things. As we grow and change, old beliefs that are inflexible break down and cease to work for us, just as an old wineskin breaks when it is filled with new wine, which then expands.

The beliefs we hold in our unconscious are called organizing principles. As we go through life, we develop principles to help us organize our feelings about ourselves and the world around us. These organizing principles operate automatically, causing us to make the choices we make and respond the way we do, and are the basis for our self-esteem.

It is only by becoming consciously aware of these unconscious organizing principles that we can make room for new beliefs. This awareness allows for growth, just as a new wineskin flexes with the new wine.[1]

WHEN AWARENESS PRODUCES GROWTH

"Neither do men pour new wine into old wineskins."
Matthew 9:17

Every time David came into my office, he was flooded with painful feelings of insecurity. He became too afraid to speak up for fear of saying something that might cause me to be unhappy with him. David's anticipation of my rejection resulted in long and painful silences in our sessions.

David had many memories of wandering into his father's study as a child and standing silently, hoping that his father would take the time to talk to him. Unfortunately, his father was often too busy to notice that David was standing there. Because David never spoke up and disturbed his father, he was never asked to leave the study. This created the organizing principle for David, "If I don't disturb people, I won't be rejected." The insidious aspect of this organizing principle was that David never tried to gain acceptance; he was constantly trying to avoid rejection. This is a task that is never completed.

After a while David became aware that he was automatically *assuming* he was going to be rejected if he said anything disturbing. Because he was so careful not to be upsetting to people, he was never open enough to find out whether or not his assumptions were correct. The result was that nothing changed for David. His shyness protected him from being rejected, but also kept him from finding out whether or not he was going to be accepted.

Things changed for David when he became aware that his fear of rejection was based on an unconscious belief. Once he became aware of this organizing principle, it became possible for David to think differently about his relationships with others. Instead of thinking, "I must keep quiet to avoid rejection," he started thinking, "I've always been afraid to speak up, but I won't *really* know how people react to me unless I do." This gave David the courage to open up to people, and he began to have much more satisfying relationships. He soon discovered that he wasn't going to be rejected every time he spoke up. In fact, many times he was able to find the very acceptance he had longed for from his father. That feeling of acceptance empowered David to grow and change in many ways. David's greater awareness directly resulted in his growth.

Jesus had an agenda. He was intent upon making others consciously aware of their relationship with God. However, he knew he was up against some obstacles. One of his biggest obstacles was the entrenchment of people in their old ways of thinking. He had to make people aware that they were trapped in old beliefs before he could get them to be open to new ones.

Human growth is vital and alive, like new wine. Jesus knew that old and inflexible beliefs, like old wineskins, break down and don't work in the presence of growth. He knew that we must achieve greater awareness of how our old beliefs need to change if we expect to enjoy the benefits of growth. As the old saying goes, "How much water can you put in a five gallon drum of oil? None. First you have to empty out some oil."

SPIRITUAL PRINCIPLE: Wise people are always discovering what they believe, even about themselves.

WHEN GROWTH PRODUCES AWARENESS

"For a tree is recognized by its fruit."
Matthew 12:33

How do you know if an apple tree is healthy and growing? By the quality of fruit it produces. Jesus knew the same is true for people. We may think we are growing, or say we are, but not really be growing at all. Or we may not think we are making much progress in life, but then find out that growth *has* taken place after we see the fruit of self-awareness it has produced in us.

Donna has been in therapy for several years. She has never had many friends, so working on herself in therapy is one of the only times in her week that she opens up to another human being. At first I thought Donna might not be very insightful. But then I came to realize that Donna did not place great emphasis upon insight. To her, actions speak louder than words.

I spend many of my sessions with Donna just listening to her. It took me a while to realize that this was exactly what she needed. I kept thinking that my insights into her life were going to be the thing that would help her change. As it turned out, she rarely seemed to benefit from those insights. What she did seem to want from me was my complete and undivided attention.

After quite some time, Donna said to me, "I was in the store the other day and it struck me. I finally realized why I am so uncomfortable standing there. I have this crazy idea that when I get up to the clerk, he is not going to like me. I finally understand what you've been trying to get me to see after all these years. I *expect* people not to like me. I get it!"

I was both relieved and somewhat embarrassed. For years I'd been trying to force-feed Donna my interpretations about her unconscious fear that people were not going to like her. But what she needed from me was simply to listen to her until she felt liked by me. It wasn't until she became comfortable, until she felt liked, that she could understand this insight. Because she had grown to believe that I could like her, she felt confident enough to grasp the insight that she was anticipating being disliked by others. Sometimes growth precedes insight.

Jesus did not espouse a philosophy as much as invite people into a relationship with him. Becoming an insightful person was not enough for Jesus; he wanted people to enter into vital relationships with God and others. To him, knowing ideas was not the same as having personal relationships.

Jesus taught that self-awareness was dependent upon feeling loved by God. He believed we could only truly understand what he was saying as a result of a personal encounter. In this way, the growth we feel as a result of being loved prepares us for the awareness of what it means to be loved.

SPIRITUAL PRINCIPLE: Self-awareness is the fruit of personal growth.

HARD HEADS COME FROM HARD HEARTS

"Are your hearts hardened?"
Mark 8:17

Even though Mrs. Adams goes to church on a regular basis, one gets the impression that she doesn't really like people very much. She is interested in becoming knowledgeable about the Bible, but she has very little tolerance for those who know less about it than she does. When discussing religious issues, her attitude seems to be that she doesn't have arguments—she simply helps people understand where *they* have gone wrong in their thinking.

One of her favorite sayings is, "God helps those who help themselves." This axiom has helped her survive in life, because she wouldn't be where she is today if she didn't believe in the virtue of hard work. The problem is that she seems to have little respect for anything else. Her family members fear that anything they do will not measure up to her standards, and the people at her church feel criticized for not being as knowledgeable about the Bible as they should be. Mrs. Adams limits her relationships with everyone she knows because she only has one way of looking at things.

There isn't anything wrong with Mrs. Adams's knowledge about the Bible. Her problem is that she's *afraid* to entertain anything new. What comes across as a kind of confidence and certainty about the Bible is actually rooted in a fear that she may not know something that she needs to know. She will spend hours quibbling with people over the Bible not because she is confident that she is right, but actually because she's afraid of ever being wrong. The narrow-minded way in which she approaches her conversations with others has more to do with what she's feeling in her heart than what she knows to be true in her head.

It isn't Mrs. Adams's love of the Bible that makes her study it so diligently; it's her unconscious organizing principle, "You must work hard to be loved." Unfortunately those who do not share Mrs. Adams's belief are often uncomfortable in her presence. If she could be open to how others might organize their lives, then perhaps she could be more accepting of them. Without the awareness that she is being guided by unconscious organizing principles rather than biblical facts, she is not likely to change.

Old wine has expanded as much as it is going to. This is sometimes a good thing. We could not function without the organizing principles we have developed from the lessons we have learned in life. But Jesus taught that *rigid* thinking is a detriment to relationships because we need to be responsive to others. He believed that narrow-mindedness is actually a problem in people's hearts, which is a way of describing something deeper than what they consciously think in their heads.

When I think, as a psychologist, of what Jesus was trying to get people to realize, I would say he was trying to get them to see that unconscious organizing principles are not bad—people just don't have enough of them. He didn't want people to throw away their old laws and beliefs; he wanted them to add new ones. He was frustrated with people who didn't want to learn anything new. People who claim to "know it all" do so because they are in the grips of unconscious organizing principles making them afraid that they don't.

SPIRITUAL PRINCIPLE: Know-it-alls need to learn about themselves.

WHY PEOPLE CAN'T CHANGE

"You are the ones who justify yourselves."
Luke 16:15

Aaron wasn't interested in therapy until after his divorce. Ironically, his ex-wife had insisted that he seek out personal therapy for years, but it wasn't until after she left that he actually did so. Aaron didn't think the problems in their marriage were entirely his fault, and so he refused to be blamed for them— which is what it felt like when she told him he needed therapy.

Aaron started his first session with me with a number of disclaimers. "My childhood was just fine," he said firmly. "I respected how hard my dad worked to provide for us, I don't hate my mother, and I've got pretty good self-esteem. I guess I'm not really sure *how* you can help me."

All I could say to that was, "You're a fortunate man. It makes me wonder why you're here."

"Well, I don't want this divorce to affect me negatively," he replied, "so I thought I would see if you could give me some advice on where to go from here."

Aaron didn't really need my advice, and he probably wouldn't have taken it anyway. What he needed was to understand himself better so that he would come up with better advice himself. *This* is where he needed my help. He thought he already understood himself as well as he needed to, so what he wanted from me was some alternative perspectives. Actually, what he needed from me was help in understanding himself better so new alternatives would occur to him. Until Aaron could come to the realization that he did not understand himself as well as he thought he did, this wouldn't be possible. It is very difficult to help individuals when they do not believe they need it.

Aaron left his brief time in therapy pretty much the same man he was when he entered it. Although he assured me he had learned a lot from our time together, I wasn't sure that he had learned much about *himself.* "Now I can say I've been in therapy," he announced proudly in our last session. "It's confirmed some things I've been thinking for a while and helped me feel better about myself." Usually I'm glad when people feel better about themselves, but not in Aaron's case. Rather than just getting a better feeling about himself, I was hoping he would get a better understanding instead.

Jesus knew that people have a tendency to "justify" themselves. We all want to think that we are doing better than average, so we tend to minimize our problems to help us feel better. But minimizing our problems isn't the same thing as facing them. Aaron's attempts at justifying himself were standing in the way of his ability to understand himself, and he wasn't going to change as long as he continued doing this.

It is very difficult to change what we don't understand. In order for us to change lifelong patterns, we have to understand ourselves better. I'm usually uncomfortable when people say things like, "Nobody knows herself better than I do" or "I've thought about my childhood and I know why I am the way I am." I find that our knowledge of ourselves is only partial, and to think we are pretty much done understanding ourselves is to put on a set of blinders that makes new growth and change of mind more difficult. The main reason people can't change is that they don't understand themselves well enough to realize where the change is necessary.

SPIRITUAL PRINCIPLE: Headway is halted by the illusion that one has arrived.

STOP LIVING IN THE PAST

"Let the dead bury their own dead."
Luke 9:60

Burt's wife insisted that he come for therapy. Because Burt was interested in being a good husband and father, he did.

"I know I'm not perfect," he said to me, "so I'd like to work on my temper. I do get angry sometimes."

"That's a good place to start," I said.

"But I don't want to go around digging up what's dead and buried," Burt continued. "I like to forget about the past and move on."

To Burt's surprise I chimed in with, "I agree with you completely. If something is dead and buried, then I see no reason for beating a dead horse."

Having heard from his wife that psychologists like to get into childhood issues, Burt didn't know quite what to say to this. Then I went on to say, "But sometimes we bury things alive."

Burt didn't realize that events in the past may still be influencing us today. We psychologists don't talk about the past because we have a morbid interest in painful circumstances that we can't do anything about. We try to understand the events of the past so we can determine the extent to which they are alive and active in the unconscious right now.

Although he didn't know it, Burt's refusal to look at his past was keeping him trapped in it. He wasn't dwelling on the past; he was living in it. Once he started looking at the painful events that went all the way back to his childhood, he started to understand the triggers for his angry outbursts. The events that he no longer carried feelings about were truly dead and buried for him. Yet things that evoked an emotional reaction for him were still alive and needed to be dealt with. Once he had made his peace with these things, he could be free to react differently when he was reminded of them. It was only then that Burt could truly say he was not living in the past and was moving on.

Living in the grips of unconscious organizing principles causes us to live in the past. It is only by examining the unconscious beliefs that were shaped by our past that we can be free to develop the new beliefs we need in our present. If we don't develop new beliefs, we have no choice but to follow the old beliefs in our unconscious. Jesus taught what psychologists believe today: that it is better to consciously choose what we believe in the present than to unconsciously follow the patterns of the past.

People who are spiritually alive are growing and learning new things. Living life out of rigid patterns from the past results in spiritual death before our physical bodies have given out. This is how the "dead" can "bury the dead." Jesus had no use for people like this. If we are to remain spiritually alive, we have to consciously develop new beliefs that come with growth.

SPIRITUAL PRINCIPLE: Those who do not learn from the past live there.

HOW PEOPLE GROW

"My power is made perfect in weakness."
2 Corinthians 12:9

Fred is a self-made man. He is well read, successful, and in good shape physically. Most people think Fred "has it all together," which is exactly what he thinks himself. Fred has become adept at eliminating negative self-talk from his life, and he is able to imagine himself coming out successful in almost any situation. Fred likes to think of himself as a "Renaissance man," able to do just about anything he sets his mind to.

Control is important for Fred. He wants to control his weight, control his emotions, and be in control of his destiny. Fred views being out of control as a weakness. To demonstrate that he is in control, Fred is constantly adding accomplishments to his life. His portfolio is getting larger, he is climbing up the corporate ladder, and he is going to night school to get another degree.

Things are improving in Fred's life, but his ability to enjoy those things is actually decreasing. His motto, "He who has the most toys wins," isn't working as well as it used to. Fred hasn't yet realized that he is actually living the same year over and over again. His circumstances are changing, but he isn't. Increase is not the same thing as growth.

Fred's need to achieve is rooted in his unconscious belief that more is better. He has never really stopped and evaluated this belief; he has simply lived it out. Each year that he has made more money, earned more degrees, or advanced past last year's numbers, he hasn't really grown at all. He has simply lived out the exact same unconscious organizing principles that he had last year; only the amounts and details of his accomplishments have been different. He hasn't been. To truly grow, Fred would have to learn something new about himself. This would require him to admit to himself, and others, that he doesn't have it totally "together," and that is too difficult for Fred.

In order for Fred to grow spiritually, he would need to admit that he can't do everything himself. To gain spiritual strength, Fred would have to be weak first, at least in his own mind. He would have to acknowledge that he needs the help of others to understand the things about himself that he cannot see. Getting better at living life from his own perspective isn't going to help Fred grow; learning how to be open to what others could teach him about himself will. Fred has always known that you won't get what you want unless you ask for it. What he hasn't realized is how to ask for what he needs.

Jesus taught that spiritual growth is not something we can do by ourselves. We need God. This isn't a sign of weakness—it's the beginning of strength. Many people would rather believe they can change by themselves than ask others to help them. This usually stands in the way of their growth.

The truth is that we cannot understand ourselves well enough alone. The unconscious organizing principles that shape our lives are primarily outside the range of our own awareness. As a result, we need someone else to point out to us the things about ourselves that we cannot see. Jesus wanted us to see that we need to ask for help in order to grow. Sometimes the only thing standing in the way is our fear that it's a sign of weakness to ask.

SPIRITUAL PRINCIPLE: Even those who get what they want must ask for what they need.

THERAPISTS AND LIGHTBULBS

"He who has ears, let him hear."
Matthew 11:15

There is an old joke that goes, "How many therapists does it take to change a lightbulb? None. It has to want to change."

Although we need others to help us grow, we must also want to. Often we don't really want to grow because that means we must look into ourselves, and we are afraid of what we might see.

Kaitlyn was raised to keep everything a secret. No one at school knew about the chaos and embarrassment going on at home. She never knew, when she got home, if she was going to find her mother passed out on the kitchen floor or if her father was going to be in one of his "moods." Not knowing how to deal with her parents' alcoholism, she simply kept everything to herself.

After a few years of being in a self-help group for adult children of alcoholic parents, Kaitlyn decided to come for therapy. She knew it wasn't her fault that her self-esteem was so low, but she felt it would be her fault if she let it stay that way.

Although Kaitlyn views herself as frightened of almost everything, I view her as courageous. Courage to me is knowing that you are afraid, but choosing to say yes to life anyway. Kaitlyn's coming to therapy was exactly that. She was very afraid of talking about her childhood; it was a nightmare she did not want to relive. But Kaitlyn wanted to make better decisions in her life, and she was determined to make use of therapy to help her do that.

At first her statement "Why do I keep doing these things?" had a self-condemning feeling to it, because she was ashamed of all the bad decisions she had made. But soon it took on an air of curiosity—she really wanted to know. As painful as it was to discuss the events of her childhood that dramatically shaped

Kaitlyn's personality, she was always willing to do it if it offered any hope that she could change.

Today, Kaitlyn isn't the same shy person she was growing up. She can concentrate on her work, can relate to others openly, and isn't attracted to dysfunctional people in the same way she used to be. Kaitlyn has grown. One of the main reasons Kaitlyn is different now is that she wants to understand how her difficult past has contributed to who she is today. She still has many fears because of her childhood, but she isn't going to let her fears keep her from understanding what she needs to know about herself. It isn't her lack of fear that makes Kaitlyn courageous enough to grow; it's her willingness to understand the things that have always made her afraid in the first place.

Jesus made a distinction between those people who were interested in changing their lives and those who were not. In his words, "He who has ears, let him hear." He assumed that everyone was able to change, and he offered people the opportunity for growth based solely upon their willingness to accept it. Growth involves a readiness to listen to ourselves and a willingness to deal with what we find there. Jesus taught that it takes courage to grow. We have to want it.

SPIRITUAL PRINCIPLE: Courage is not the absence of fear, but faith in spite of it.

SOMETIMES YOU CAN'T GO BACK HOME

"Only in his hometown and in his own house is a prophet without honor."
Matthew 13:57

When Emily came for therapy she was concerned about her inability to deal with her relationships at work. She viewed herself as insecure and ineffective with people. We soon came to see that Emily's first feelings of ineffectiveness were with her mother. It was with her that Emily first began to believe that she was a burden to other people. If you believe your own mother finds you a burden, then it is not a stretch to assume that everyone else views you the same way.

Emily was in the grips of the unconscious organizing principle, "My feelings are a burden to others." This unconscious belief caused her to be tentative in all of her relationships. The result was that most people never knew where Emily stood, and so they had a difficult time relating to her. Unfortunately, Emily's belief became a self-fulfilling prophecy.

Over the course of our therapy together, Emily became aware of her unconscious organizing principle. Once it was made conscious, she did not experience it in the same way. Although Emily still found it difficult to express her feelings to others, she no longer automatically assumed that they were a burden. This change in Emily's perspective allowed her to be much more open and effective in her relationships.

Almost everyone was interested in the new way Emily was relating to them, except for her mother. Emily's ability to be open about her feelings became very disruptive to the relationship with her mother. As Emily began to speak up about how she felt, including the things that disturbed her, she found herself in more arguments with her mother than ever before. Emily now had opinions.

"Is this what you're learning in therapy? How to blame everything on your mother!" her mother would say.

"Can't I disagree with you without you feeling attacked by me?" Emily would reply. These arguments rarely came to a satisfactory conclusion for either of them.

Although Emily had always been uncomfortable around her mother, she was now more aware of it. She didn't want to feel this way about her mother, nor did she want her mother to be uncomfortable around her. Emily's mother was still acting as though Emily's feelings were a burden to her. Emily needed her mother to come to this realization before things could change, but Emily's mother wasn't aware that anything was in need of change. As Emily worked harder at trying to get her mother to see the need for change, her mother only became angrier at Emily for doing so.

Emily and her mother needed a new relationship. Emily was still her mother's daughter, but she wasn't her child anymore. Because Emily had changed her perspective on her own emotions, she had changed the rules of the relationship with her mother. She no longer unconsciously believed her emotions to be a burden. She now needed her mother to believe this as well. What Emily's mother saw as disrespectful and argumentative, Emily saw as painful feelings that needed to be discussed. Emily was desperately trying to make things better with her mother, but the way her mother saw it Emily was trying to tear their relationship apart.

Now that Emily has changed, she can never go back to the way things were with her mother. Sometimes you can't go back home. She isn't giving up on her relationship with her mother; she is simply insisting on a better one than the one they had before. Change is coming very slowly, but Emily feels that both she and her mother are worth it.

Jesus taught that once people embarked on a relationship with God, they could never look at the world in the same way again.

Sometimes spiritual growth means a radical change in perspective. This kind of shift in outlook has consequences for relationships. Jesus learned in his own life that a "prophet" cannot return home.

Once people are able to make unconscious organizing principles conscious, they never look at the world in the same way. Going to therapy can result in making us more aware and can change the way we perceive the world for the rest of our lives. Sometimes our friends and family are happy to see us grow and change, and sometimes they are not. When the people around us are not happy to see us change, going home can become an uncomfortable thing to do.

SPIRITUAL PRINCIPLE: Change is an unwelcome guest in the home of familiarity.

GROWTH IS WORK

"Shoulder your cross, and follow me closely."
Mark 8:34 (Living Bible)

The process of growth does not erase our original organizing principles. We still remember the past even if we don't choose to live in it. Under the right circumstances, we can even be tempted to respond in the same old ways. Our brains still have the same neural pathways as before waiting to be stimulated again with the right cues. We can't change our old organizing principles into new ones, but we can learn to rely upon new organizing principles until the old ones fade into a distant memory. Jesus taught that growth involves hard work. We must be prepared to shoulder our part of the responsibility if we expect to reap the rewards.

Megan came back to therapy because she saw a dissatisfying pattern in her life in which she kept dating needy men who expected her to be their cheerleader. Because Megan had been in therapy before, she knew her "cheerleader" approach to life was the result of her relationship with her father, who was seriously depressed. Because she was his favorite, she always felt responsible for his happiness and consequently never allowed herself to be in a bad mood in hopes of cheering him up.

"I want to change," she said to me. "I've had it with these losers. I want to rid myself of all the baggage of the past and move on. Where are all the decent men?"

Feeling as though I was being called upon to be a cheerleader for Megan, I paradoxically responded with, "You can't change, but you can grow."

Megan didn't like hearing this, and it took us several months to unpack its meaning for her. The truth is, the unconscious organizing principles that Megan established throughout her childhood are a permanent part of her unconscious terrain. Neither of us can change that. She is probably going to feel something every time she meets a man who reminds her in some way of her father. What *can* change is Megan's response to her past. Now that she is conscious of the fact that she felt responsible for her father's feelings, she doesn't have to keep acting as though this is still true. Each time she is tempted to "take care" of another needy man, she can ask herself if she is responding to the needs of the man in her life *now* or the man who *was* her life years ago. She can grow into the awareness that she can care for the man in her life without having to "take care" of him. Responsibility means "ability to respond," and acting automatically out of unconscious principles from the past removes her ability to respond and replaces it with an obligation to react in the same way she always has.

When Megan was saying "I want to change," she was really saying "I can't stand how this feels anymore, and I want the bad feelings to go away." Growth is about moving toward good feelings, not trying to escape bad ones. We can't erase Megan's organizing principles, but we can help her develop new ones. She can learn that the needs of men in her life today are *opportunities* for her to respond, not *requirements* that she must meet. Although this means Megan must still be aware of how she was hurt by her father's depression, she is better able to grow past its effect on her because of that awareness.

Jesus talked about the process of spiritual transformation as a task we need to embrace over and over again every day. When he invited people into this process, he instructed them to "shoulder their cross" because he knew it involved work. He did not see the better life as an escape from bad feelings. He didn't offer people instant change. He saw the better life as embracing the difficult job of following him closely. The by-product of this life is continual growth.

SPIRITUAL PRINCIPLE: Quick changes are often temporary, but slow growth often lasts.

CHAPTER 4

UNDERSTANDING SIN AND PSYCHOPATHOLOGY

"There was a man who had two sons. The younger one said to his father, 'Father, give me my share of the estate.' . . . Not long after that, the younger son got together all he had, set off for a distant country and there squandered his wealth in wild living. . . . When he came to his senses, he said, . . . 'I will set out and go back to my father and say to him: Father, I have sinned against heaven and against you.' . . .

"But while he was still a long way off, his father saw him and was filled with compassion for him; he ran to his son, threw his arms around him and kissed him. . . . The father said to his servants, 'Quick! . . . Let's have a feast and celebrate. For this son of mine was dead and is alive again; he was lost and is found.'"

Luke 15:11–24

In the parable of the prodigal son, Jesus tells us that the main cause of sin is selfishness. The primary result of sin in the parable is not necessarily debauchery, but getting lost. The prodigal son went off in his own direction and ended up alone, and lost. The father in the story doesn't mention the wild living that depleted his son's inheritance. He doesn't even consider the son's behavior in need of punishment. This parable isn't about fiduciary responsibility;[1] it's about the solution to sin in the world. Jesus was making a point. Sin is self-centeredness that results in a broken relationship, and salvation is the moment that relationship is restored.

Making yourself God is at the core of both spiritual and psychological problems, because both sin and psychopathology are the result of self-preservation at all costs. This chapter is about how sin and psychopathology are caused by broken relationships and how salvation and psychological health occur when relationships are restored.[2]

THE PATHOLOGY OF SELFISHNESS

"If you cling to your life, you will lose it."
Matthew 10:39 (Living Bible)

Dora stopped believing in people a long time ago. Her parents failed her, her friends failed her, and God hasn't come through for her either. Dora has come to believe if you want something done, you have to do it for yourself.

Dora sees other people as adversaries. It's as if she is competing with everyone for everything, and she wants to make sure she doesn't get ripped off. The problem is that even if she succeeds in keeping others from cheating her out of what she wants, she still feels cheated. If you don't have people with whom you can share, getting what you want isn't satisfying for very long.

Dora has built up a wall of defenses to make sure no one can take advantage of her. What she doesn't realize is that she not only has walled others out; she also has walled herself in. The truth is Dora is angry because she is alone. In trying to save herself from the victimization of others, Dora has created her own hell. She tries to protect herself by mistrusting others, heal her hurts by isolating herself, and plan for the future by fighting for what she wants. Dora doesn't have many friends because she is so defensive around others, and her life doesn't feel meaningful because she doesn't believe in anything bigger than herself.

Dora acts as though she is absolutely certain about what she wants, and it is generally useless to argue with her about it. But Dora's façade of confidence doesn't come from feeling good about her life; it actually comes from the opposite. Dora is so busy trying to keep things from getting worse that she is making it impossible for things to get better. What Dora doesn't realize is that keeping others at a distance may make her feel safe, but it prevents her from getting what she needs to feel whole. Both psychologically and spiritually, Dora has lost her way, and without the assistance of others she won't be able to find what she really needs.

The beginning point of both salvation and psychological health is the recognition of our need for others. Spiritually speaking, we need a relationship with God to be whole. Psychologically speaking, our mental health depends upon our ability to relate to others. If we see others as adversaries we must protect ourselves against, we become defensive and run the risk of damaging the very thing we are trying so hard to protect.

Jesus taught that humans are relational beings. He often spoke about the importance of our vertical relationship with God and our horizontal relationships with each other. To Jesus, spiritual health is what happens when relationships are intact and sin is what happens when relationships are broken.

When we become afraid that we are not going to get our needs met, we engage in emergency acts of self-preservation, or defense mechanisms, to protect ourselves. These defense mechanisms unfortunately become the psychopathology that separates us from others as well as from our own true selves. Jesus taught that humans cannot exist as islands; psychologists teach that we can't be whole without relationships with others. Both sin and psychopathology result from desperate acts of self-preservation, which makes selfishness at the core of both spiritual and psychological problems.

SPIRITUAL PRINCIPLE: Selfishness is sin *and* psychopathology.

HEALTH AND SALVATION ARE MOVEMENT
TOWARD OTHERS

"Just as you can hear the wind but can't tell where it comes
from or where it will go next, so it is with the Spirit."
John 3:8 (Living Bible)

I once attended a lecture by a cultural anthropologist who explained why certain cultures in the world could not understand American missionaries' descriptions of Christianity. His explanation was that in America we think in terms of bounded sets. He represented this by drawing a series of circles on the board to demonstrate how we think of people as belonging to certain groups and not others. Christians are inside one circle, and non-Christians are outside of it. If you enter into the circle of Christianity, then you are saved. If you don't, then you aren't. When American missionaries try to get others to join their circle, they have difficulty if those people don't also think in terms of bounded sets.

The way some cultures think of Christianity has more to do with relationships, which can be represented by a cross surrounded by a series of arrows of various sizes pointing in all directions. If the cross represents Jesus, then you are a Christian in these cultures if your arrow is moving toward the cross. It doesn't matter how big your arrow is, how close it is to the cross, or even how long it has been there. All that matters is that you are approaching the cross now. I believe Jesus had something like this in mind when he told the parable of the prodigal son. He was saying that sin is moving away from a relationship with the Father, and the solution to sin is to reverse our direction and move toward him.

I have always believed that therapy is a process of spiritual movement. Neither the therapist nor the patient may be aware that God is present, but this does not restrict his ability to create movement in our lives. When my patients perceive a lack of this movement in therapy, that is, when they don't feel that things are going well, they refer to themselves as "stuck." Then when things begin to make sense to them and they feel therapy is effective, they say things like, "Now we're getting somewhere." Although most patients don't really have a good idea of where they want to go, they do want to be getting somewhere as quickly as possible.

Derek came to therapy as a very motivated man. He was genuinely interested in improving himself and making use of therapy as a resource. However, he approached therapy with a bounded-set way of thinking. He wanted me to tell him what he was doing wrong, and then he would simply correct his behavior. He believed there was a circle of mentally healthy people, and he wanted to get inside it. When we would come to insights about Derek's life, he seemed genuinely pleased to come to this new knowledge about himself, but he rarely seemed satisfied with this achievement. He would typically follow moments of insight with, "That sounds great. Now what should I do?" I don't believe Derek was trying to be difficult; I truly believe he was viewing mental health as a set of behaviors he was trying to identify and acquire for himself.

Like all of us, Derek is a product of his culture. He even started his therapy with me with the question, "How long do you think this will take?" When people ask me this question, I typically think I'm going to be in for some difficulty. The metaphor I usually respond with is working out at the gym. When do you ever get done working out? Everyone seems to understand the necessity of integrating physical exercise into our lives on a daily basis. That we need to maintain the capacity for physical strength and movement seems obvious. Working out emotionally is really the same thing. The goal isn't to get done—it's to get stronger. In the terms of this metaphor, a psychotherapist is much like a trainer. We never get done with a need for working out physically or emotionally, but at some point most of us no longer need our trainer to be with us every step of the way.

Derek stopped feeling stuck in his therapy, and in his life, when he stopped viewing mental health as something that he could achieve. He started feeling better about himself when he began viewing mental health as a way of approaching others. He's less concerned now about getting on the inside of some fictitious group of people and is more concerned about how he relates to the people already in his life. Derek rarely asks me what I think he should do anymore, because he no longer believes that there is one right answer to this question.

Jesus taught that sin is anything that separates us from God and others. This was his point in the parable of the prodigal son. If we're moving toward God, then we're moving in a spiritual direction. If we are moving away from God, then we're moving in an unspiritual direction. This is why the father in the parable was ready to throw a party at the mere sight of his son moving in his direction.

Jesus talked about the Spirit of God being like the movement of air. To his Hebrew way of thinking, God was described as a verb. This meant that God was active and godliness required action. For Jesus, wholeness could only be achieved through making movement toward God.

One of the spiritual truths of psychotherapy is that the goal is not to arrive, but to be making movement. It isn't arriving inside the circle of mental health that indicates success in therapy; it's developing the capacity to make movement toward others. Those patients who understand this truth make the best use of therapy and can understand why the prodigal son's father threw him a party.

SPIRITUAL PRINCIPLE: In Jesus' language, God is a verb.

THE ROLE OF REPENTANCE IN THERAPY

"Repent and believe the good news!"
Mark 1:15

Dr. Smith came for therapy as a result of an ultimatum from his wife. He was a successful surgeon, but unsuccessful as a husband. His wife complained constantly about him, and going to therapy was his chance to turn things around. He was coming because he felt bad about his relationship with her, and he didn't know what else to do.

Surgeons must be very precise in their work. Dr. Smith was hard on his nursing staff for a very good reason: people could die if they made mistakes. Unfortunately the same rigorous adherence to precision that made him a success at work was undermining his success at home. Dr. Smith felt bad about his wife's unhappiness in their marriage, but he saw her complaints as illogical and largely unsubstantiated by the facts in their marriage. He was faithful, a good provider, and always supportive of their children's needs. He even saw himself as open to changing his views on anything she was upset about if she could show him where he was off in this thinking.

Even though I had been seeing Dr. Smith for several months, our real therapy began long after we had our initial session together. Dr. Smith's therapy began when he had a change of mind. During one session when we were struggling with his wife's complaints about him, Dr. Smith exploded out of frustration with, "Why won't she lay off? Do I have to spend my whole life with somebody on my back?"

"I don't know," I said. "Have you always had somebody riding you?"

"Yes," he said as his face turned red. "Nothing I ever did was good enough for my father, and now all I get is the same crap from my wife. How perfect do I have to be?"

The light came on for Dr. Smith. Working harder made him a better surgeon at the office, but the same strategy wasn't working at home. He needed to work differently. He wasn't really trying to be happy in his marriage; he was trying to avoid feeling bad. He was using the same strategy he had learned as a child to avoid his father's criticism. He thought if he just worked harder and did things better, he wouldn't get in trouble. He began to wonder if he ever did anything because he *wanted* to do it. Perhaps everything he did was to keep others from being unhappy or disappointed or even dying. This was an exhausting way to live. He wasn't seeking happiness; he was constantly avoiding its opposite—a never-ending task.

Dr. Smith changed his mind. He decided he didn't want to keep living his life based upon the dictum, "I live to avoid the criticism of others." He needed a new motto. He wanted to start doing things because he truly wanted to do them. But in order to know what you want, you have to know how you feel. Dr. Smith had a new reason to come to therapy. He wasn't coming to figure out how to keep his wife from being unhappy with him anymore; he was coming to try to figure out how to be happy himself. He stopped trying to get help to change her and started trying to receive help to change himself. This is the role of repentance in psychotherapy.

Ironically, Dr. Smith's wife doesn't complain as much about him anymore. The more he has become interested in his own feelings about things, the more he talks about his feelings with his wife. As it turns out, she wasn't that interested in his doing things better; she just wanted to know how he felt about the things they were presently doing.

Most people think repentance is feeling bad about themselves after they have done something wrong. Repentance to them is a kind of self-punishment or guilty feeling that one deserves for doing something one shouldn't have done. Jesus didn't see it that way. Even though the wayward son in the parable of the prodigal son feels bad and insists he has sinned against his father, Jesus portrays the father as oblivious to these guilt feelings and only interested in one thing: his son has changed his mind and come home. According to Jesus, the son's act of repentance occurred not when he begged his father for forgiveness, but when he decided to change his life and return home. Feeling bad about himself didn't make a difference—changing his mind did.

The Greek word for "repentance" in the Bible is *metanoia*, which means "change of mind." It means being on a path in one direction and then deciding to reverse your direction to go on an entirely new path. Jesus talked about repentance in this sense. He didn't want to make people feel bad about themselves; he wanted to help them change. This is the same thing therapists want when patients come to them for therapy.

Repentance plays a role in psychotherapy if we define repentance in the way that Jesus did. Jesus saw repentance as the time when you change your mind and stop trying to do things your own way. In therapy, you must see the need for change in order for it to work. Both spiritually and psychologically, you must have a change of mind in order to grow.

SPIRITUAL PRINCIPLE: The wise are always prepared to change their minds; fools, never.

TRUE VERSUS FALSE GUILT

"He will convict the world of guilt . . ."
John 16:8

Many people think that a psychotherapist's office is where they can go to be relieved of their guilt. They believe that guilt is neurotic, and therapists are specially trained to help them out of it. After all, whatever they are feeling guilty about probably wasn't their fault to begin with, and they believe that psychologically healthy people don't waste time crying over spilled milk.

Chip approached his sessions with me with the same enthusiasm and charisma he applied to all the areas of his life. He was articulate, motivated, and successful at everything he did. Although Chip assured me that he loved his wife, he reported an indiscretion: he had had an affair. His wife was furious with him once she found out, insisting that he go to therapy to figure himself out. Chip was genuinely disturbed by the possibility that his marriage was about to fail. He hated to fail.

Although Chip was very clear with both me and his wife that he felt terrible about what he had done and that he wanted to make his marriage work, I found myself having difficulty helping him. It was obvious to me that he felt bad, but it wasn't obvious why. Eventually I came to realize that Chip did feel guilty, but he didn't feel bad about what he had done—he felt bad about being caught. The type of guilt that Chip felt was not based upon the remorse that comes from hurting someone you love; it was based upon a fear of the consequences for screwing up. What Chip was feeling was false guilt.

It is hard to treat false guilt in psychotherapy because things are not as they appear to be. Chip knew he felt bad about his affair, but he couldn't admit to himself why. If he were honest with himself, he would probably admit that he didn't really believe men were capable of monogamy and that "spicing up" a marriage with a little extracurricular activity was probably a good thing from time to time. But Chip couldn't admit these things because he knew what his wife, and probably I, would think about them, and he was afraid of what would happen to him then.

Chip left therapy after a few months feeling much better about himself. He reported to both me and his wife that he was glad he had come to therapy and he had learned a good deal about himself. Chip never did agree with me about the nature of his guilt feelings, and in fact he thought my approach to therapy was a little obsessed with *feelings* anyway. He advised me to look into more solution-oriented approaches to treatment like the kind he'd heard about on the talk-radio stations. "The important thing," Chip would say to me, "isn't to sit around feeling bad about the past. It's to make the most out of what you have today. She's just going to have to get over it someday and trust me again. It's time to move on."

As far as I know Chip was successful in avoiding a divorce, but I doubt if his wife ever felt safe in their marriage. It is possible to move past false-guilt feelings, but unless they are acknowledged for what they are, the underlying fear that caused them is never resolved. Although things seemed better, both Chip and his wife continued to live with the feeling that something was not quite resolved.

Even though Jesus said he did not come into the world to condemn it (John 3:17), he did believe there are times when we should feel guilty. From his perspective, not all guilt is bad.[3]

Jesus believed in two kinds of guilt. What psychologists call true guilt, he would call guilt based upon love. What we call false guilt, he would say is guilt based upon fear. True guilt is the remorse we feel when we hurt those we love; our conscience makes us want to make things right in our relationships with others. False guilt is the fear of punishment that is more concerned about protecting ourselves when we have done something wrong.

False guilt isn't concerned about others, and it rarely helps our relationships with them. In fact, it is usually self-defeating and makes us more difficult to be around. We feel true guilt when our relationships matter to us and we are motivated to heal the wounds that need our attention. This is the kind of guilt Jesus wanted us to feel.

SPIRITUAL PRINCIPLE: Guilt motivated by love heals hurt; guilt based on fear only hides it.

IF PEOPLE WERE PERFECT, WOULD ANYONE SIN?

"Be perfect, therefore, as your heavenly Father is perfect."
Matthew 5:48

Melissa gets excellent grades in school, her teachers love her, and her room is spotless. Who could ask for more from a kid in junior high? Melissa appears to everyone to be the perfect child.

But surface appearances can be deceiving. Melissa has friends, but only if they play the way she wants them to play. Sometimes the kids call her bossy. Actually, Melissa prefers the company of adults. She always gets attention for her intelligence and poise. What most people don't realize is that Melissa's appearance of being advanced for her age is actually a need for control that covers over deeper problems. Melissa isn't the perfect child because she *enjoys* being that way; Melissa is a perfectionist because she *must* be that way.

A number of children with self-esteem problems slip through the educational system undetected because they never cause problems. It's the noisy and unruly kids who get identified as having problems, while the overperfectionist ones sit silently in their seats going unnoticed. But inflexibility can be just as much a sign of low self-esteem as acting out to get attention. Perfectionism is just a more socially desirable way to deal with it.

Being perfect has never been a sign of mental health. Quite the opposite. Having the courage to be imperfect is more a sign of healthy self-esteem than pretending to have it all together. Children like Melissa sometimes work so hard to get attention for being good because they are afraid they won't be loved if they don't. If children don't feel loved for who they are, they take attention shown them for what they do as a substitute. It's the next best thing. The issue isn't whether or not their behavior is perfect; it's their motivation for their behavior in the first place.

Occasionally I come across verses in the Bible that disturb me. One of those verses is, "Be perfect, therefore, as your heavenly Father is perfect." This sounds as though Jesus was setting a ridiculously high standard for his followers, which, if not met, might make them feel sinful and inadequate. Over the centuries many people have confused moral perfectionism with spiritual righteousness and have defined spirituality by the number of things from which they abstain, such as smoking, drinking, and swearing. But sometimes it is the very people striving to be perfect who are the ones most guilty of sin.

The Greek word translated as "perfect" in this passage can also be translated "mature."[4] Once I learned this I felt a lot better. I know I won't ever be perfect, but I do believe I can continue to grow. Maturity means acknowledging that we will continue to sin. Pretending to be flawless is actually a sign of immaturity. Jesus didn't define spiritual maturity as the absence of imperfections, but rather as the presence of strength.

The wisdom of Jesus is that we cannot earn love; we can only receive it. Trying to be perfect morally or behaviorally does not make us any more worthy of God's love. Unconditional love is about who we are, not what we do. People with healthy self-esteem feel this way about themselves. As I have come to understand the teachings of Jesus, we do not feel more loved because we are perfect—we desire to become more mature because we feel loved.

SPIRITUAL PRINCIPLE: Perfectionism is a guise, not a goal.

WHEN BEING RIGHT IS A SIN

*"If any of you causes one of these little ones who trusts in me
to lose his faith, it would be better for you to have a rock tied
to your neck and be thrown into the sea."*
Matthew 18:6 (Living Bible)

Nancy is a very intelligent and outspoken woman who can't keep
herself from getting angry when the conversation turns to religion. She is well versed on all the atrocities that have taken place
throughout history in the name of God. Nancy would never
admit it, but she is actually quite religious. She isn't agnostic,
holding that we cannot know if there is a God. She is an atheist,
which means she actively *believes* there is no God. This requires
faith.

Nancy is quite convinced that there is no God because this is
what she learned from her childhood. The ironic part about this
is that both of her parents are very religious people and actively
involved in their church. Nancy grew up going to church every
Sunday, memorizing her Bible verses along with the other children, and trying to be as good as possible because she believed
that then God would bless her.

Unfortunately, by the time Nancy was thirteen her parents were
divorced. The fact that her parents got a divorce wasn't what really
hurt Nancy; it was the way they went about it. The two godliest
people she knew were transformed into two of the most bitter and
vengeful people she could imagine. Both of her parents kept going
to church regularly, and in fact they started talking more about
God than they ever had before. But now Nancy's spiritual conversations with her parents centered around pouring over the Bible to
find justifications for why one parent or the other was "out of
God's will" and why each parent's anger toward the other was
actually righteous indignation. Neither of them had lost their religion, but what they had lost was their love.

Nancy's father changed to a different church and eventually remarried. Nancy's mother told her that her father was living in sin and cautioned her to learn from his mistakes. Nancy's father referred to her mother as a fundamentalist and told her there was a special place in hell reserved for people like her mother, so Nancy would do well not to follow in her footsteps. Not knowing whose religious views to believe, Nancy decided not to believe either of them. Both of her parents believed they were righteous because they believed they were right. Whether or not relationships had to suffer because of it was secondary.

Nancy hates religion because of the religious people who make being right more important than their relationships with others. Ironically, Jesus had similar feelings. On one occasion he ranted about the religious leaders of his day with, "Woe to you, teachers of the law and Pharisees, you hypocrites! You are like whitewashed tombs, which look beautiful on the outside but on the inside are full of dead men's bones and everything unclean. In the same way, on the outside you appear to people as righteous but on the inside you are full of hypocrisy and wickedness" (Matt. 23:27–28). Nancy isn't an atheist because she finds it intellectually satisfying to be one, but because it allows her to blame religion for what happened to her parents. The truth is she feels a knot in her stomach from hating religion and secretly wishes everything could return to how good it felt when she was a child. In terms of the impact upon Nancy's life, her parents' need to be right turned out to be very wrong.

Jesus had very harsh words to say to those who hurt children. Our selfish need to be right at the expense of those who depend upon us is a crime Jesus considered worthy of punishment by being "thrown into the sea." Being right is never more important than the well-being of children. Hurting them is always a sin.

SPIRITUAL PRINCIPLE: No adult is right when a child's faith is wronged.

IS SELF-DENIAL SPIRITUAL MATURITY OR PSYCHOLOGICAL HANDICAP?

"If anyone would come after me, he must deny himself and
take up his cross daily and follow me."
Luke 9:23

Jesus taught unconditional acceptance in the parable of the prodigal son, but at other times he taught about the necessity of self-denial for all who desired to follow him. Both are important in the life of the spiritual person. To understand this apparent contradiction, we must comprehend the difference between the true and false self.

The true self is the image of God within each human being, which desires a relationship with God and others. The false self is the constructed image we create for ourselves to deal with the world around us; it is defensive and self-protective. When Jesus spoke about unconditional acceptance, he was referring to the true self, our essence that is in the likeness of God. When he spoke about the denial of the self, he was referring to the false self, our selfish outer shell that makes intimacy with God and others more difficult. In order to relate spiritually and authentically with one another, from true self to true self, we must be able to set aside the false self.

Jacob wanted to succeed in his career as an attorney, but he felt insecure about his natural ability to be persuasive with others. He compensated by staying late at the office doing excessive amounts of research and attempting to be better prepared than his opponents. Jacob always "went by the book" in his dealings with others and would never take credit for anything that wasn't his. He believed his hard work would win him his cases, because he didn't believe he deserved it otherwise. Jacob always put other people first, because he was too uncomfortable to do it any other way. He often found himself doing work for his associate, Connor, because he had a difficult time saying no.

Connor also wanted to succeed in his career as an attorney, but he believed that his social skills made him irresistible to others. He was certain that he could persuade anyone of anything, given enough time. Connor had no problem taking credit for Jacob's work and cutting corners whenever possible, because he believed only the strong survive in life. If he *could* get Jacob to do things for him, then why *shouldn't* he? He wasn't holding a gun to his head.

On the surface, it may look as if Jacob's self-denial is more spiritual than Connor's arrogance. It is true that Connor is in denial about his abusiveness toward Jacob, and his false-self entitlement to take advantage of others is the kind of selfishness that Jesus wanted us to put to death. But self-denial is different from low self-esteem. Jacob suffers from a false-self devaluing of who he truly is. Jesus was not interested in getting people to undervalue themselves; he was trying to get them to view themselves accurately and to live out of that self-perception. Jacob's false-self *devaluing* of himself can be just as damaging to his relationships with others as Connor's false-self *overvaluing* of who he thinks he is. Neither man was offering his true self to others, which takes a lot of work. Jesus told people they would have to "take up the cross" to follow him because living authentically is just that hard to do.

Jesus called us to deny our false selves so we could authentically follow him. This type of self-denial is both spiritually and psychologically healthy. When we lower our defenses and relate authentically, we affirm our true selves and become more of who we were created to be in the first place.

SPIRITUAL PRINCIPLE: A persona renounced is a person revealed.

SIN IS A PERSONAL PROBLEM

"If your brother sins, rebuke him, and if he repents, forgive him."
Luke 17:3

Jesus talked about sin as "missing the mark" or making a mistake.[5] But he wasn't as concerned about the mistakes people made as he was about the broken relationships that *resulted* from those mistakes. This is why he was quick to forgive people. To him, the relationship was the problem that needed our focus. Focusing on the mistakes people make misses the point.

Laila and Kerry were friends. As friends often do, they shared personal information about their lives with each other. Laila didn't think it was necessary to explain to Kerry which things were confidential and which were not, because she thought it was obvious. Unfortunately, what's obvious to one person may not be so obvious to another. Not thinking she was betraying a confidence, Kerry shared the details of an intimate conversation they had had with another mutual friend. When this got back to Laila, she was furious with Kerry.

Laila decided she couldn't trust Kerry anymore and began saying unkind things about her to their mutual friends. It was as if she were trying to balance the scales of personal pain between them. Laila had been hurt by Kerry, so she felt entitled to say things that might hurt her in return. "She deserves it," Laila would say to herself whenever she said something unflattering about Kerry, "after what she's done to me."

When Kerry learned of the things Laila was saying about her, she was shocked. Kerry couldn't believe she had been so open with someone she thought was her friend. "How could I have been so stupid," Kerry thought. "Laila is only interested in making herself look good at the expense of others. She's no friend of mine."

The tension between Laila and Kerry soon became well known to everyone around them. No one really knew why they disliked each other so much, but it was clear that they did. Laila and Kerry kept the feud going because they were asking the wrong question. The issue wasn't "Who started it?" but "Who's keeping it going?"

Kerry had "missed the mark" with Laila and made a mistake. Laila had a right to be hurt and angry about that. But to Jesus, the issue with sin isn't what was done in the past, but what can be done now to resolve it. Laila and Kerry kept the sin going because they were both more concerned with protecting themselves than healing the wrong between them.

"The things that cause sin are bound to come," Jesus said, "so watch yourselves" (Luke 17:1–3). Then in the next breath he says, "If your brother sins, rebuke him, and if he repents, forgive him." His focus was on restoring personal relationships. Jesus often took the psychological perspective of focusing on sin not as a problem within people, but as a problem *between* them.

SPIRITUAL PRINCIPLE: Sometimes sin is a problem between people, not within them.

WHO GOES TO HELL?

"How will you escape being condemned to hell?"
Matthew 23:33

Human beings experience a constant battle between sin and spirituality as well as between psychopathology and psychological health. For most of us, the battle is either unconscious or not that extreme. For some, however, the battle is both conscious and extreme. It is then that we start using such terms as "evil" or "sociopath" to describe someone who is beyond cure. When confronted with a choice between good and evil, these people condemn themselves to hell.

Ted Bundy murdered over thirty people. He was arrested, escaped twice, and was eventually executed in Florida. He was intelligent, was socially skilled, and at times could be charming. Bundy understood people, but he had no compassion for them. He saw people as objects to be manipulated rather than as human beings with whom he could have relationships.

Bundy was abused as a child, and he never dealt with the effects of that abuse. He developed feelings of inferiority that he covered over with an attitude of entitlement. He wanted to have power over others and lost his ability to relate to them as persons. Each time Bundy engaged in an act of cruelty toward another, any hope for the capacity for guilt feelings was buried deeper in his unconscious. Tragically, at some point Bundy became addicted to acts of horror the way a drug addict medicates himself against painful feelings. The feeling he received from killing became his drug. He had no feelings toward others; he only cared about the feelings he could generate for himself. Bundy lost touch with his humanity. His own psychological life was more important than the physical lives of those he used. This is an extreme case of self-preservation at all costs.

Some people cross over the line in their abuse of others and act without a conscience, or capacity for feelings of remorse. Those who cross over this line enter into the soulless world of sociopathy. We may not be able to know exactly where that line is, but because of people like Bundy we do know it exists. We can't help these people because they don't want it. People, like Bundy, do exist for whom, for all practical purposes, there is no cure.

Some people never find a cure for their psychopathology. As a result of some combination of environmental influences and genetic biology along with the lack of opportunity to find the right psychological help, they never find relief from psychological suffering. Theoretically, I believe there is at least some help for everyone who seeks it out, but some people have to find just the right therapist before it's too late for that help to be effective.

Jesus taught that not everyone would be saved (Matt. 13:41–42). Even though everyone was invited, not everyone was going to accept the invitation to enter into a spiritual relationship with God. It grieved Jesus deeply (Luke 19:41), but he recognized that some people could not surrender their position as god of their own lives. These people create hell on earth and never escape.

SPIRITUAL PRINCIPLE: Those who create hell for others end up there themselves.

SALVATION AND PSYCHOTHERAPY

*"For this son of mine was dead and is alive again; he was lost
and is found."*
Luke 15:24

"I think I have a broken picker," Sarah said to me in our first session.

"Picker?" I asked.

"Yes, you know, whatever makes me pick the men I do must be broken. Can you fix that?" she asked.

As a therapist, I could detect in this opening line both good news and bad news for Sarah. It was good that Sarah wanted to look at herself—that makes therapy promising. But it was not good that she thought there was something defective about herself. I have found the *belief* that one is defective more damaging than any actual defect that might be discovered.

As our therapy progressed, I learned that Sarah's parents had divorced when she was in grade school and that her mother had to get a job to support her and her sisters. Sarah had turned to the other children at school for the attention she needed because her parents were no longer around to provide that for her.

By the time Sarah got to high school, her relationships with boys had turned sexual, and sexual intimacy became the price she paid for the feeling of closeness she needed. Sarah came to believe that the only way she would get what she needed was to give others what they wanted in return. This kind of conditional love left Sarah with the feeling that she could get attention for what she did, but she didn't know if she could get love for who she was.

It took a long time before Sarah knew how to relate to me in therapy. For a while she imagined that we might have a sexual relationship at some point. Then she thought I was only seeing her for the money she paid me and that I secretly found her disgusting because of her past sexual activities. But after many hours of telling me the worst things about herself and opening up to me the darkest and most unacceptable aspects of her life, Sarah began to think that it might be possible for another person, a man, to be interested in her for some reason other than what he could get from her in exchange. Sarah was rediscovering her true self, the part of her that desired to have an unconditional relationship with another for who she was, not what she did.

The things Sarah had done to find love were not evidence of some personality defect in her; they were attempts to find lost love. Sarah had not gone back far enough in her history to find the explanation for why she was the way she was. Her sexual promiscuity didn't provide an explanation for who she was; it was an unfortunate result of a need that went unmet. Once Sarah found the little girl inside who longed for a father's love, her life started to make more sense. She wasn't defective—she was unloved. The little girl who was once lost had been found again, and Sarah felt as if she was coming home to who she truly was.

Sarah doesn't need to keep acting as though there is something wrong with her. The problem wasn't with *her;* it was with what she needed and didn't get. Because Sarah is starting to feel less like there is something wrong with her, she is starting to believe that what she has to offer is more valuable. Not too surprisingly, Sarah is attracting a different kind of man as well.

Jesus taught that sin is separation from God, and salvation is a restored relationship with him. In the parable of the prodigal son Jesus was saying that salvation from sin is coming home where we belong.

Psychotherapy works because it follows the pattern that Jesus describes for the process of salvation. Relationships heal us. We cannot be psychologically healthy without having healthy relationships with others. Human beings were created that way—we must be connected to others to be whole.

Psychotherapy is a process of helping people who are lost find their way back home. By establishing a relationship in therapy we therapists can help our patients discover how they have become derailed from healthy development, and by assisting our patients in the development of healthy relationships with us, and others, we can get them back on the track of psychological health.

SPIRITUAL PRINCIPLE: A lost soul is found, not fixed.

C H A P T E R 5

UNDERSTANDING RELIGION

At that time Jesus went through the grainfields on the Sabbath. His disciples were hungry and began to pick some heads of grain and eat them. When the Pharisees saw this, they said to him, "Look! Your disciples are doing what is unlawful on the Sabbath."

He answered, "Haven't you read what David did when he and his companions were hungry? He entered the house of God, and he and his companions ate the consecrated bread— which was not lawful for them to do, but only for the priests. Or haven't you read in the Law that on the Sabbath the priests in the temple desecrate the day and yet are innocent? I tell you that one greater than the temple is here. If you had known what these words mean, 'I desire mercy, not sacrifice,' you would not have condemned the innocent. For the Son of Man is Lord of the Sabbath."

Matthew 12:1–8

Jesus believed that religion was made for people, rather than people made for religion. Even though it was a violation of Jewish law for Jesus to do what he did on the holy day of the Sabbath, he did so anyway. He said things like, "Which is lawful on the Sabbath, to do good or evil, to save life or to kill?" (Mark 3:4). Jesus often confronted those who had become rigid in their thinking and lost sight of the purpose of religion.

Psychologists have observed that just as children's ability to grasp more abstract thinking develops as they grow, so does their ability to grasp moral complexity. Both intellectual and moral development grow from the more concrete to the more abstract. This means that as we mature, we come to realize that rules exist as guidelines to facilitate better relationships between people. Jesus placed the spiritual practice of mercy above the religious practice of sacrifice; this is very similar to what psychologists say about moral development.[1] Mercy always considers the other person; sacrifice can sometimes be just for ourselves.

RELIGIOUS RITUALS

"Do this to remember me."
1 Corinthians 11:24 (Living Bible)

Katherine and Brandon came for marital counseling to improve their marriage. They knew they loved each other and they were proud of the way their children were turning out, but things could be better between them, and they both knew it.

Katherine was from an emotionally expressive family and was used to open displays of affection as well as anger. Brandon's family was much more reserved. From his perspective, talk was cheap; it's your actions that count. Katherine was frequently trying to engage Brandon in conversations about his feelings so she could feel loved in the way she was used to. Brandon, however, was busy trying to demonstrate to Katherine that he loved her by how hard he worked at things without having to talk about it.

"Sometimes I just need to know how you feel," Katherine would plead.

"I married you, didn't I?" Brandon would typically respond. "Who do you think all of this is for?"

Over the course of our therapy together, we discovered a helpful ritual for Katherine and Brandon's marriage. Brandon was comfortable taking action to demonstrate his feelings, but he needed to act in ways that communicated meaningfully to Katherine. He knew when Katherine was unhappy, but he often didn't know what to say to help her. It was at those times that Brandon began the ritual of the loving hug. The hug wasn't to communicate a desire for sex or to avoid the conversation; it was simply to send Katherine the message that he loved her.

After talking about it, Katherine and Brandon decided that the loving hug had become an important ritual to help them through difficult times. Sometimes they didn't have the words to deal with how they were feeling, and it was at those times that the loving hug could communicate a meaningful connection between them that they both desired. Just as Jesus intended rituals to be used to remember God, so too we can use them to remember our love for each other.

A ritual is a concrete action symbolizing a spiritual reality. Jesus believed that religious rituals were a good thing when used to help us remember that we have a relationship with God and others, even at times when it is hard to do so. As humans, we tend to forget. Rituals give us something tangible to help us with the intangible nature of our relationships.

Jesus knew that we all have times when we need something concrete to help us remember that our relationships are real. Sometimes we need physical evidence that love exists, and concrete rituals can serve as that evidence. Religious rituals can be a good thing, as long as we remember their purpose.

SPIRITUAL PRINCIPLE: Rituals help us remember love.

THINGS GET GRAYER AS WE GROW

With many similar parables Jesus spoke the word to them, as much as they could understand.
Mark 4:33

Jonathan's parents divorced when he was in grade school, and he only saw his father on weekends. He remembers sitting outside his mother's place waiting for his dad to come and pick him up. It always hurt when his dad was late. His mother didn't help matters with comments like, "Well, I guess your father just has more important things to do than be with his own son." Jonathan hated that feeling of being unimportant to his dad. To his child's mind it was simple, "If he loved me, he would be here when he said he would."

Today, Jonathan insists on being punctual. He is never late if he can help it, and he expects the same respect from everyone else. Jonathan has come to believe that being late has only one meaning in life—the person who's late just doesn't consider the other person important enough. Jonathan is very concrete about the meaning of being late.

Jonathan's precision about time has extended to other matters in his life. Being accurate about facts, always telling the truth, and keeping promises (no matter how small) on the part of others are all indications of whether or not they find him important enough. He has ended friendships over single incidents of imprecision in these areas. Jonathan demands precision from his friends because that is the only way he can know if they value him.

Unfortunately for Jonathan, he hasn't realized that being respectful of another's time, accurately telling the truth, and keeping promises are only symbols of how much we value other people; they are not the proof. There are many reasons we may fail to be precise with our time, words, or deeds. Because of Jonathan's early pain in these areas, he is stuck at a concrete level of symbolization. To him, precision doesn't *symbolize* that another person is important; it concretely *proves* it. Jonathan has lost several relationships and continues to feel hurt unnecessarily, because he is so concrete about his understanding of punctuality. Jesus intended symbolism to be a good thing because it can enhance relationships; he never thought it should be used to tear them apart.

Jesus believed religious symbolism was helpful to people at all levels of education and intelligence. He always spoke in parables so that people could extract the meaning from his teachings that was applicable at that time. Giving people concrete images to focus on helped them understand more abstract spiritual principles. Jesus was a master storyteller because he knew the power of symbolism in communicating ideas.

A spiritual person is a growing person, one whose perception of the world is constantly evolving from the concrete to the abstract. Things that were once "black and white" become "shades of gray" as we grow. Jesus instituted religious rituals to help us remember him, not because the rituals themselves were magically able to empower us. Some people get stuck at the concrete level of understanding and miss the purpose of religious rules and rituals. Following religious rules and rituals for their own sake, without understanding their purpose of facilitating better relationships with God and others, is empty religion that robs people of spiritual life.

SPIRITUAL PRINCIPLE: Rituals aid love; they do not replace it.

WHY FREUD HATED RELIGIOUS FUNDAMENTALISM

"They were harassed and helpless, like sheep without a shepherd."
Matthew 9:36

Dylan came to therapy because his marriage was falling apart, and his friends told him it might be a worthwhile thing to do. He was friendly and liked to talk, but he had a hard time figuring out why he should be in therapy. He saw himself as a fun-loving guy who had simply married a woman who was too uptight about things, especially his drinking. "I just made the wrong choice. What can I say?" was his explanation for the problems in his marriage.

Over several weeks of sessions and after much prodding and searching on my part, Dylan and I came to an important discovery. He wasn't just interested in having fun; he was deeply invested in not feeling bad. In fact, Dylan was so focused on not feeling bad that he would medicate himself with alcohol in order to avoid painful feelings whenever possible. Although Dylan was trying to convince himself he was a social drinker going through some bad times and thus drinking too much, he finally came to the realization that he was an alcoholic. I never told Dylan he was an alcoholic; it was a term he came to use for himself.

Over the next year, Dylan transformed. He began attending AA meetings, stopped drinking, and became rather religious. He had not been interested in religion since the few years he spent in parochial school, but something had changed for him. Dylan could admit that he was helpless to do certain things in life now and that he needed God to help him. He could talk about his inadequacies, open up to emotions he never knew he had, and trust other people for the first time in his life. Dylan's realization that he was helpless and that he needed God changed his life. Dylan would tell you that God quite literally saved his life, and he's not the least bit shy about telling people that his religion has made him a more genuine man.

Freud hated religion. I don't think it's necessary to go into Freud's religious upbringing and what caused him to be so angry with religion, but he called it an illusion people used to defend against their feelings of helplessness in the world.[2] In this view, people live superficial lives, hiding behind religious rituals and rules instead of facing deeper meanings and feelings. Some people do in fact do this, primarily religious fundamentalists.[3] But in Dylan's life, religion was having the opposite effect that Freud thought it would.

Jesus disagreed with Freud's view of religion. To him, acknowledging our helplessness was a sign of spiritual maturity, and turning to God for help was the very best thing to do. Religion isn't supposed to be a defense against helplessness; it's a vulnerable response to helplessness that opens us up to a relationship with someone who can help us when we need it. To Jesus, we are all helpless and in need of God.

SPIRITUAL PRINCIPLE: Health begins with recognition that you are not God.

WHY JESUS HATED RELIGIOUS
FUNDAMENTALISM

*"Woe to you, teachers of the law and Pharisees, you
hypocrites!"*
Matthew 23:27

Although Jesus would disagree with Freud's conclusions about
religion in general, he would agree with the specific criticism of
religious fundamentalists who use it as a defense. Jesus hated the
inauthentic use of religion. Jesus saw religion as a structure to
make a relationship with God easier, not a rigid set of rules that
makes people feel good, or bad.

Noah and Rachel's marriage was in trouble. Noah had had an
affair. He ended up in a compromising situation with a woman he
had known for years, and they made love. He felt terrible about
it and wanted to figure out how such a thing could happen to
him and his marriage. Although it only happened once, he felt he
needed to confess it to Rachel and ask for her forgiveness. Rachel
was furious.

As a devout Christian, Rachel was offended that Noah could
defile their marriage bed. He had committed the one sin that
gave her biblical grounds for divorce, and she intended "to be
obedient to the Word of God." Noah was repentant, but he was
also confused. He didn't believe that his act of unfaithfulness was
merely the result of weak willpower on his part; he also thought
it was a manifestation of something wrong in their marriage.
Rachel saw this as evidence of an unrepentant heart and threatened him with a divorce.

Marriage counseling was difficult because Rachel was convinced she was the innocent victim of a sinful act of immorality,
and Noah wasn't sure he knew what was going on. Rachel had
become an expert in biblical verses on infidelity and marriage
vows, and she used them liberally in our counseling sessions.

"If you would spend more time in the Word, you wouldn't fall prey to such things," Rachel would offer as a solution. "Then you would have known your body is not your own."

Noah would often just look down, not knowing what to say next.

Although Noah and Rachel decided to stay together, the marriage counseling ended somewhat unsatisfactorily for all of us. For Noah there were two issues: the forgiveness he needed for his sin against his wife and the problems in their relationship that had caused him to look elsewhere. For Rachel there was only one issue, and anything Noah said that tried to turn the focus of attention back on her was an indication of his unwillingness to take responsibility for the sins of his flesh. He had sinned against her, and she expected him to spend the rest of his life making it up to her. She had the biblical right to leave him if she ever wanted, and if she chose to she would exercise her right with a righteous indignation.

Jesus considered infidelity a sin and something hurtful to relationships. But for him, the Holy Scriptures were to be used to enhance relationships with God and others, not to give us leverage over them. People sometimes believe they have scriptural evidence that they are right, and yet they are spiritually wrong. Rachel was using her religion as a defense against looking at her contributions to her marriage problems, and it was never intended to be used for that purpose. This is the kind of religious fundamentalism that both Jesus and Freud might agree makes rules more important than people and only gets in the way of life as it is intended to be lived.

Jesus didn't think being religious was a problem, but he did have concern for the way some people approached religion. When religious rules become more important than the people who follow them, religion can become toxic. It was offensive to Jesus when people took something that has the potential to unite people with God and others in a life-giving way and used it to distance themselves from painful feelings of inadequacy by artificially enhancing their estimation of themselves through false piety. To Jesus, religion was something that produces vulnerability and connection, not something that produces grandiosity and religious pride.

SPIRITUAL PRINCIPLE: True religion raises up God, not us.

THE PROBLEM WITH RELIGION

"I desire mercy, not sacrifice."
Matthew 12:7

Mrs. Johnson is a social worker who oversees child-abuse cases, and she takes her job very seriously. Her caseload is larger than those of her associates, and she works longer hours because she is a "type A" personality who has an obsessive need to pay attention to details. Although Mrs. Johnson is not a religious person, she is religiously dedicated to her job.

Hannah is a new social worker who was recently hired to work for Mrs. Johnson and who is eager to get started in her career. She doesn't have the type of personality that focuses on details like Mrs. Johnson's, but Hannah feels she has chosen the right career path because of her love for children. Hannah is idealistic about her work as a social worker, and she hopes her optimism will help when the work gets difficult. Hannah has a religious passion about her work with children.

Unfortunately, Mrs. Johnson doesn't like Hannah's ideas and approach to social work. Mrs. Johnson believes she needs to protect the field of social work from dreamers like Hannah who don't understand what hard work it is to protect children through a complicated and difficult social system. "You can't read about this in books, and life here isn't a fantasy. The only way to become a good social worker is to spend time in the trenches and pay attention to details," Mrs. Johnson was fond of saying.

Because Mrs. Johnson didn't like Hannah, things became more difficult as time went on. She disciplined Hannah every time she made a mistake in her paperwork, she constantly criticized her decisions with her cases, and she never missed an opportunity to correct Hannah when it came to office policy. Eventually, Hannah left her job feeling discouraged and overwhelmed. "I guess I'm just not cut out for this type of work," she said on her last day. "You people have a different attitude toward life than I do."

The tragedy was that Hannah might have become a good social worker if she had had the necessary encouragement. But because she wasn't going to turn out to be a social worker in the mold of Mrs. Johnson, Hannah wasn't acceptable. Mrs. Johnson sacrificed a lot for her job, and so she felt entitled to decide who should be allowed to succeed there and who should be discouraged from staying. Tragically, her sacrifice was less out of compassion for others than out of a rigid need to follow the rules. People can be religiously rigid about many things in life; in Mrs. Johnson's case it was her job. Jesus taught that wherever people are rigid, someone is going to pay a price. Unfortunately, that someone in this case was Hannah.

Throughout history many people have engaged in various forms of sacrifice as a part of their religious practice. Setting aside one's own desires for the benefit of another can be the sign of true compassion when it is motivated by love. But sacrifice without love is hollow religion.

Jesus believed that religion without love is religion without substance. This is why he desired "mercy, not sacrifice." How we practice our religion makes all the difference. Rigid adherence to religious practices that loses sight of their purpose, which is to connect us to someone outside ourselves, is bad religion. Jesus loved religion, but he hated rigidity. Religion isn't the problem, but the rigid practice of it robs people of their souls.

SPIRITUAL PRINCIPLE: Religion isn't a problem; religious rigidity is.

THE CONSERVATIVE FUNDAMENTALIST

"The Son of Man came eating and drinking, and they say,
'Here is a glutton and a drunkard, a friend of tax collectors
and "sinners."'"
Matthew 11:19

I knew I was going to be in for a difficult time with Matthew from our first session. "Are you a Christian?" "Where do you go to church?" "What do you think about prayer?" "What is your theoretical orientation?" These were just a few of the questions that came at me. These can actually be good questions, but the rapid-fire manner in which they were coming at me caused me concern.

It soon became apparent to me that Matthew was trying to find out as much as possible about me because he needed to know if we were different in any way. This prospect seemed very threatening to him. I would answer his questions honestly, and he would seem temporarily satisfied with my answers, but before long he would pursue some additional avenue of questioning to see if he could uncover some difference between us. It was as if he had already decided he should be afraid of me and he needed to find out why.

Matthew was more concerned about why other people did what they did than he was about understanding himself. We spent quite a bit of our time discussing how his wife had failed to live up to his expectations and a fair amount of time talking about how his co-workers were living immoral or irreligious lives by his standards. Matthew was almost obsessed with measuring other people's behavior, and of course they always came up short.

Although it was difficult for both of us, Matthew and I did make some progress in therapy. We were able to shift the focus of our investigation onto Matthew, probably not as much as I would have liked but probably more than he really wanted.

Matthew started to see that he was being judgmental at times toward his wife and that that was not a good thing. He could admit that he required a high degree of conformity from others before he could feel comfortable. And just before we terminated our treatment, Matthew was starting to take a closer look at how his approach to religion was playing a role in these matters.

Matthew's strict adherence to rules and his measuring of other people's behavior were his attempt to use religion to defend against his fears that he might not be adequate in God's eyes. If he could be assured that all true believers acted exactly the same as he did, then he would know he was acceptable to God. If anyone was different, then he might be in trouble and not know it. Everyone who was right needed to be the same in order for Matthew to feel safe. Although Matthew never did surrender this belief totally, we may have opened the door to his looking at it in the future.

Conservative fundamentalists are extremely rigid about the rules of religion because that is the way they can know if they have a relationship with God. At the deepest level, their spiritual life is based upon a heartfelt desire to relate to God, but their inflexibility leaves no room for individual differences, and anyone who disregards their rules of religion becomes threatening to them. From this perspective we must all follow the specific, concrete rules of religion in order to have a relationship with God. If we don't follow the rules, we lose the relationship.

Jesus loved people. He loved to be with them in their homes, visit their places of business, and go to their parties. He wasn't considered a truly religious person by the conservative fundamentalists of his day because he placed being with people above rigidly following religious rules. So they called him a "glutton, drunkard . . . and friend of sinners." Jesus knew that true religion was not a matter of conformity—it was a matter of the heart. He loved the differences between people, and he saw no need to eliminate those differences in order for people to be religious.

Jesus believed the strongest practice of religion involved the participation of many different kinds of people all working together to form a common bond of fellowship based upon their love for God and each other.

SPIRITUAL PRINCIPLE: True community isn't conformity—it's love.

THE LIBERAL FUNDAMENTALIST

"A student is not above his teacher, nor a servant above his master."
Matthew 10:24

Andrew is a very intelligent man. Our sessions together can at times take on the quality of intellectual discussions more than psychotherapy. It wasn't easy earning Andrew's confidence at first, because I had the feeling that Andrew had to be sure that I was intelligent enough to help him. He would ask me what famous authors I had read and pose philosophical questions about which we could muse.

Although it was important for Andrew to feel that we were intellectually compatible, he was quite comfortable with the fact that we were also different. I think to this day Andrew believes that he is at least slightly more intelligent than everyone else. This is a difference between himself and other people that he secretly enjoys.

Andrew considers himself to be very open-minded, which is why he hates conservative thinkers. He considers traditional religious views and conservative theology the source of many injustices over the centuries. He thinks following stringent religious rules is a nonthinking approach to life, and he believes this rigidly.

But Andrew doesn't come to therapy for help with his thinking. He comes for help with his despair. Although Andrew is involved in a number of meaningful causes and activities in his life, he is constantly dealing with low-grade depression. Andrew thinks his life is meaningful, but he finds it overwhelming. It is a difficult burden believing you are smarter than everyone else, because along with that belief comes the feeling of responsibility to do something with it. Andrew believes in God, but only as an abstract concept. He has been disappointed by those he has looked up to so often in life that he doesn't really even trust in God. He has found trusting in the power of his own intelligence to be more reliable.

Andrew is actually quite inflexible about his beliefs, even though his beliefs are liberal ones. People don't normally think of Andrew as a fundamentalist because he isn't conservative. But the truth is, Andrew is a liberal fundamentalist. It's not the content of his religion that makes him a fundamentalist; it's the rigidity with which he holds his beliefs. Andrew is intolerant of intolerance.

The liberal fundamentalist doesn't believe in following concrete rules in the practice of religion and adhering to strict beliefs. This type of fundamentalist looks down on the conservative types as unthinking sheep who must conform to petty rules because they don't have the intellectual ability of their more liberal brethren. Liberal fundamentalists have unknowingly replaced God with the brilliance of their own minds. After all, the truly enlightened aren't expected to follow the same rules the common masses need, are they?

Jesus taught that intellectual superiority was not a requirement for spiritual maturity. He often confronted educated fools. Worshiping one's own mind is an insecure religion; there is no one else to turn to in times of need. Often liberal fundamentalists are outwardly motivated to change the world, but secretly despairing because it is up to them to accomplish it. Jesus wanted religion to be a vehicle through which we receive God's help in our lives, not a vehicle through which to help God.

SPIRITUAL PRINCIPLE: True comfort is never found in the god of one's own mind.

THE PURPOSE OF RELIGION

"First go and be reconciled to your brother; then come and
offer your gift."
Matthew 5:24

Many years ago, I went to the county jail with a friend of mine
named Vern to talk to the inmates there. My friend did this on a
regular basis, and he invited me to go along one Sunday after-
noon to experience a side of life that would be different for me.

When I arrived at the jailhouse, I was not permitted to enter
without Vern. The sheriffs had watched well-meaning souls come
and go over the years attempting to provide compassionate support
for the prisoners, but experience had told them that they would
never last. Vern was the only person allowed to visit the jail without
their supervision because he had demonstrated the ability to stick it
out with this population. This was not for the faint of heart.

Vern had a regular routine at the jail. He would walk up to
each cell, give its inhabitant a small green Bible, and ask him if he
would like to talk about God. If the inmate agreed, he would
launch into a dialogue on the benefits of a relationship with God
in terms only prisoners could understand. I thought Vern had the
foulest language of anyone I had ever met before. Although I was
somewhat shocked at the time, I look back on it now and realize
Vern was speaking their language.

I'll never forget Vern standing there in the jailhouse in his outdated leisure suit speaking to the prisoners in his coarse and
uncouth language. I doubt that Vern would be popular in most
religious circles, given his appearance and mannerisms, but fortunately that didn't seem to matter much to him. He wasn't religious in order to fit in with traditional religious groups. Vern's
religion was his relationships with the prisoners, the sheriffs, and
God. Everyone had nothing but the highest respect for him, and
I think that was especially true for God.

I think back on my experience with Vern, and I'm grateful for the opportunity to have witnessed a man living his religion. Jesus knew that some people use their religion, but others live theirs. He never intended religion to be used to get us social standing, networking opportunities, or power over others. It was intended to bring us life. It was clear in the teachings of Jesus that if religious practices ever got in the way of our relationships with others, then we were to set aside our rituals and repair our relationships first. His priority was clear, "First be reconciled to your brother."

The religion Jesus intended is meant to connect us to God *and* each other. There is no "getting ahead" or rising above others; there are only deeper connections. We are to worship God and respect each other. The respect of each other on the horizontal level was the spiritual parallel to the worship of God on the vertical. To Jesus, the corporate practice of religion was intimately tied to each person's personal religious practices. On the spiritual plane we're all one.

SPIRITUAL PRINCIPLE: Religion would be fine if it weren't for the people, which is also why it exists.

THE PURPOSE OF RELIGIOUS RULES

"Do not think I have come to abolish the law."
Matthew 5:17

Psychologists who have studied human moral development have come to an interesting conclusion. We begin in life with very concrete rules for dealing with moral dilemmas. We *must* follow the rules. As we advance in years, we become more abstract in the way we deal with morality. The more morally mature people are, the more they realize that rules are guidelines to be followed, not rigid laws that must be obeyed.

At first this may sound as if the higher people move up the ladder of moral development, the more they only do what they want to do for themselves. Ironically though, research has shown that at our highest level of moral development we humans consider not only our own needs, but those of others as well. Psychologists have found people at the highest level of moral development to be altruistic. In the lives of the few people who have been considered to achieve the highest stages of moral development we are now able to observe what Jesus taught—rules exist to help us love.

The Tompkinses called me for help because their teenage daughter, Amanda, was out of control. Amanda is an exceptionally bright child and was a model student in school up until two years ago. Now she was failing most of her classes, truant from school more than in attendance, and constantly in trouble for her aberrant behavior. The dream child had become a nightmare.

One of the tragedies of the Tompkinses' nightmare was that Mr. and Mrs. Tompkins were extremely loving and kind people. It seemed so unfair for such good people to struggle with such bad behavior from their child.

As we talked about the distress in their family, I discovered that Mr. and Mrs. Tompkins had an unspoken definition of love that seemed to be contributing to the problem. They had both been raised by authoritarian parents who were strict and punitive in their discipline. Because this felt unloving, both Mr. and Mrs. Tompkins decided to exercise discipline in their own family in ways distinctly different from the ones in which they had been raised.

"All I knew when we got married is that I didn't want to be anything like my father," Mr. Tompkins explained.

"We've always tried to be fair with Amanda," Mrs. Tompkins chimed in. "She never even needed spanking as a child. We don't understand where she learned this kind of disrespectful behavior. It certainly didn't come from us."

The Tompkinses were trying to be as loving as possible with Amanda, but their definition of love was to try to be and do the opposite of what they had experienced as unloving in their own childhoods. They thought love should be boundless, which inadvertently led them to try to love Amanda without boundaries. They thought they were being respectful of Amanda by allowing her to make her own choices about her clothes, bedtime, and use of the telephone when she was growing up. They thought she would only feel loved by them if she knew they trusted her judgment. But what they didn't realize is that love needs boundaries as well as respect and trust.

Through the help of therapy the Tompkinses were able to establish some rules for their relationship with Amanda. The privileges that Amanda enjoyed brought with them the responsibility to adhere to certain family rules regarding behavior, along with consequences if she failed to live by those rules. Speaking respectfully to each other, honoring a curfew, and following through with commitments such as going to school and doing designated chores were spelled out clearly. At first, Amanda was furious with her parents. But in time, things began to change. Amanda's attendance at school improved, she spent less time in the principal's office, and her language around the house became more civil. The most important change in Amanda, though, was that within a few weeks she actually seemed happier. Ironically, the rules that everyone in the Tompkins household were trying to avoid actually became the very things that helped them be more loving toward each other. The Tompkinses discovered the ancient truth that Jesus preached a long time ago. When used appropriately, rules exist to help us love.

Jesus taught that the highest form of human development is to love others. Although this is a state of being to aspire to, it is not easily achieved. All religions contain a set of rituals or rules that are used to structure the religious activities of the participants. The religious rules that Jesus practiced served the purpose of making the love of others something that could be aspired to by all. To him, the commandments of God existed to help human development achieve its highest state, the capacity to "love one another."

SPIRITUAL PRINCIPLE: When love is the law, we police ourselves.

THE KEY TO A MEANINGFUL LIFE

"Therefore be as shrewd as snakes and as innocent as doves."
Matthew 10:16

Ethan has always been afraid of something. During his childhood he was afraid he was going to get picked on at school, he would wake up with a wet bed, and there really was something scary in his closet that only came out at night. Unfortunately, Ethan wasn't very good at talking about his fears growing up so he didn't get much help with them. He was pretty much on his own to come up with strategies to deal with his fears.

Ethan's best strategy for calming himself down when he became afraid was to count. He would count the checks on his pajamas, the lines on the floor, or the number of times he would turn out the light before going to bed. Somehow it made him feel as if he were in control of things when he counted. Since no one else was going to protect him, Ethan would use his ability to count to protect himself.

The problem with Ethan's strategy of counting is that it didn't really protect him from danger; it just made him *feel* as if he were doing something to protect himself. It was a concrete symbol of protection rather than the real thing. Because of this Ethan couldn't help feeling afraid shortly after having finished counting, so he would have to count some more. By the time Ethan came for therapy he was in the grips of numerous counting rituals that were firmly entrenched in his life. He couldn't stop counting. It was as if his life depended upon it.

As a result of quite a bit of therapy and some helpful medication, Ethan doesn't count as much as he used to. He has come to the realization that his counting ritual was a helpful symbol of safety that he needed to survive the scary, lonely times he went through as a child. The problem was he never saw it as a ritual that had deeper meaning. It was a magical act he needed to do to protect himself. Now that Ethan understands that the rituals in his life have deeper meanings, he is better able to employ strategies other than counting to protect himself when he feels afraid. Because of this, Ethan doesn't feel afraid as often as he did before. Ethan would tell you that his life feels more meaningful in a number of ways now because he is looking for the deeper meanings behind all the concrete actions in his life. Ethan thought he was being smart about things by counting before; now that he understands the meaning of his counting ritual, he finds that he doesn't have to count much at all.

Jesus taught that religion, and life itself, is meaningless unless we understand its symbolism. Life should be a mixture of concrete rituals and abstract experiences. The key is to make use of the concrete to facilitate deeper meanings. As a psychologist, I think this is part of the perceptiveness that Jesus was talking about when he encouraged us to be "shrewd as snakes." The meaningful life gets to the core of things and doesn't stay at the superficial level of understanding.

Jesus believed that religion can bring great meaning to our lives as long as we use its rituals as tools to deepen our understanding of ourselves and God. We must strive to understand the abstract meaning hidden within the concrete rules. This is the key to a meaningful life.

SPIRITUAL PRINCIPLE: Pray for a soft heart and a sharp mind.

CHAPTER 6

UNDERSTANDING ADDICTION

A certain ruler asked him, "Good teacher, what must I do to inherit eternal life?"

"Why do you call me good?" Jesus answered. "No one is good—except God alone. You know the commandments: 'Do not commit adultery, do not murder, do not steal, do not give false testimony, honor your father and mother.'"

"All these I have kept since I was a boy," he said.

When Jesus heard this, he said to him, "You still lack one thing. Sell everything you have and give to the poor, and you will have treasure in heaven. Then come, follow me."

When he heard this, he became very sad, because he was a man of great wealth. Jesus looked at him and said, "How hard it is for the rich to enter the kingdom of God! Indeed, it is easier for a camel to go through the eye of a needle than for a rich man to enter the kingdom of God."

Luke 18:18–25

Some people have difficulty relating to God, but because they have a fundamental need to relate to *something*, they substitute objects instead. This is Jesus' definition of idolatry. He knew that the rich ruler had to surrender his worship of wealth before he could make room in his heart for a relationship with God.

Some people have difficulty in their relationships with other people. When their relationships are threatened or lost, they substitute objects in their place. This is the definition of addiction. The ancient problem of idolatry is manifested as the modern problem of addiction. As the rich ruler discovered, once objects have been substituted for relationships, it can be very difficult to surrender them.

Turning to an object to cover over our unmet need for love can work—temporarily. The euphoria that comes from possessing certain objects can make us forget that we are in need of something deeper. But because an object is only a substitute for the love we get from our relationships, its satisfaction never lasts. We must return again and again to the object to ward off our feelings of emptiness and dissatisfaction. According to Jesus, an idol is a substitute for love because it is an attempt to replace a relationship with an object. An addiction is a substitute for love for the very same reason.

Confronting people who feel unloved and have turned to addictions can be helpful, but only for a time. Reassuring people who are in this situation can also be helpful, but this too is limited. Only one thing heals human addiction and drives out idolatry: genuine love. Human beings are never satisfied unless they experience the real thing.

ADDICTION AND IDOLATRY

"Where your treasure is, there your heart will be also."
Luke 12:34

Tim was a bright, successful entrepreneur who came to therapy because his wife insisted that they get help for their relationship. There weren't any obvious problems like excessive fighting or disagreements about finances or the children. Their marriage just seemed flat. I soon discovered that the reason Tim's wife wanted more from him was because he was "checking out" at crucial points in their relationship by drinking enough scotch to take the edge off of the conversation. His perspective was that this was his way of relaxing and dealing with the stresses in his life. Her perspective was that he was covering over his feelings, which she desperately wanted to know.

I suggested to Tim that he try an experiment. My idea was that he discontinue his drinking while they were in therapy so that they could deal with all of their feelings. Tim agreed, but he could only manage to do this for a few days at a time. When his feelings built up to the point where he would have to deal with them, he couldn't resist the temptation to fall back into his pattern of drinking to make them seem more manageable.

As often happens in cases like this, the marriage therapy began to go flat too. If people can't bring in all of their true feelings, then even the best therapy can't help much. The turning point for my therapy with Tim came when I told him that I didn't think therapy was going to help him as long as he continued to drink. I don't say this to everyone, but I was convinced that this "thing" was standing in the way of the most important relationship in his life. Unfortunately, Tim couldn't stop. I suggested that he go to an AA meeting, but he refused. Rather than dealing with his feelings with his wife or me, Tim turned to scotch instead. Even though he never could admit it, his drinking had come to occupy such a place of importance to him that psychologically it had become an addiction and spiritually it had become his god.

I don't know how things eventually turned out for Tim because he terminated therapy before he could change. Like the rich ruler in Jesus' parable, he just walked away. We do have the choice between "things" and relationships. When we choose "things," we surrender our lives to gods that enslave us rather than set us free.

Jesus didn't have a word for addiction, but he understood that when we set up "gods" that demand our attention to the exclusion of our relationships with others in life, we get into trouble. His word for that was idolatry.

Jesus said something to the rich ruler that he never said to anyone else about how to get into heaven. He said, "Sell everything you have and give to the poor." Jesus wasn't interested in the man's "things"; he was interested in getting the man to see that his "things" were at the center of his own interest. The man had substituted "things" for a genuine relationship with God. He had become addicted to his idols.

SPIRITUAL PRINCIPLE: Any substitute for love never lasts.

STINKIN' THINKIN'

"No one is good—except God alone."
Luke 18:19

Substituting a concrete thing for relationships with others requires some mental gymnastics. Addicts must come up with numerous rationalizations for why they don't have a problem, and they will try to convince you, and themselves, that they are only interested in having a good time. The truth is they are using the objects or substances they are addicted to to avoid the bad times. Alcoholics Anonymous calls this "stinkin' thinkin'," which is using intellectual rationalizations to avoid emotional pain.

Samantha and Kevin came for marital counseling because they were trying to decide what to do about having children. They had been trying to conceive for some time, and nothing was happening. Samantha wanted Kevin to get medically checked out, but Kevin was dragging his feet about making an appointment. On the surface they claimed to be quite happy and in agreement about things, but their behavior indicated otherwise.

Early on in our counseling I discovered that Kevin had an answer for everything. He appeared good-natured and always had a cheerful reply to any situation. When Samantha would confront him about making a doctor's appointment, he always had good reasons why this wouldn't be a good week. He would reassure her that next week he would take care of it first thing.

The more we talked, the more I discovered a number of other things that didn't quite fit either. Kevin's performance at his job was rather poor. He explained that this was due to inadequate support staff and an unreasonable boss, which was all going to change. He would stay up late at night claiming he just couldn't sleep and miss early morning appointments, but none of that was really a problem for him. Samantha and Kevin always seemed to have financial problems. Kevin explained he was a "people person," not a "numbers guy," so they couldn't evaluate exactly where their money slipped away from them. Samantha believed that part of loving someone is trusting them, so she never questioned Kevin's explanations, and, besides, he always seemed so sincere in his response. She thought he needed her to help him be less chaotic in life, and she never suspected him of being dishonest.

As it turned out Kevin *was* being dishonest, but it was mostly with himself. Kevin had a drug problem, but he couldn't admit it. He saw himself as a good person and a fun-loving guy. Sure, he liked to party as much as the next guy; everyone in his line of business did. He didn't see that as a problem. When he would use drugs at home alone, he would tell himself that he was just trying to deal with the pressures from work, on the one hand, and Samantha's harping about having a kid they couldn't afford, on the other. Kevin was in denial about the fact that his drug use was hurting his performance both at work and at home. He could see how everyone else might have problems, but he couldn't see it in himself.

Kevin was trying to convince everyone that things were "good" when they weren't. He made looking good more important than dealing with the feelings he was having with Samantha. Things started to turn around for Kevin when he came to grips with the point that Jesus made with the rich ruler. No one is good except God, so don't even try to pretend otherwise. We all have problems, so take the emphasis off of trying to look good and put it on trying to have good relationships with God and others. Once Kevin came to grips with this, our real therapy could begin.

Jesus knew that people need to appear to have it all together because they are afraid they don't. When Jesus replied to the rich ruler, "Why do you call me good? Only God is good," he was telling him that he wasn't interested in helping people look good; he was interested in helping them find a relationship with God. He knew this guy was into appearances. Because the man was well-to-do, Jesus went straight for what he knew to be the man's true god. Even though the man believed himself to be righteous, substituting physical things for emotional relationships was still idolatry, no matter how good he could make it look with rationalizations.

SPIRITUAL PRINCIPLE: Emphasizing looking good makes it harder to be it.

THE PROBLEM WITH DRUGS

"It is easier for a camel to go through the eye of a needle than
for a rich man to enter into the kingdom of God."
Luke 18:25

The reason people can't just quit their addictions is because addictions work—temporarily. Turning to something concrete that produces a reliable effect over and over again gives people a sense of security. They can make the pain of not getting their intangible needs met go away. Relationships are not reliable; they change and place demands upon us. Concrete things are always the same; we know what to expect.

However, the satisfaction that comes from using material things as substitutes doesn't last. Eventually the pain of our unmet needs begins to resurface, and we then think we know what we can do about it. We return to our concrete solution, but gradually find that it isn't enough. Because it isn't a genuine solution but only a substitute, we begin to need more and more of it. Yet something inside of us knows that it isn't what we really need, so we increase the intensity of the substitute to do a better job of covering it up. This is why addiction is referred to as a progressive disease.

I played football in high school with Ricardo. The interesting thing about Ricardo was that he was the most mild-mannered, polite person off the football field and the most violent, aggressive person on it. It was as if his personality transformed once he donned his uniform, like Clark Kent changing into Superman. I knew Ricardo well enough to know that he came from an abusive home life. He had a lot of painful things to cover up in his life, and he was doing an excellent job of it. Looking back on it now, I think I know where all the violence that he unleashed upon opposing players came from.

Ricardo was cool. He was a gentleman, well dressed and highly regarded by everyone. All the guys respected him because of the reputation he had earned on the football field, and all the girls admired him because of his sophisticated mannerisms. Most of us knew that Ricardo smoked dope, but somehow he made even that seem cool. He was always in control and able to deal with any situation that presented itself. If you ever got into trouble, Ricardo was the man to get you out of it. Everybody wanted to be known as a friend of Ricardo.

Several years after graduation I returned to my hometown for a visit. I looked up Ricardo for old time's sake, hoping to recount football stories and nostalgic memories. I was excited to see him and looking forward to our discussion. Tragically, I couldn't have been more disappointed. Apparently Ricardo's drug usage had escalated, and he had moved on to harder substances. Even though it was ten o'clock in the morning, he couldn't stay alert enough to hold a conversation. His mind wandered as we talked, and he often didn't make much sense. He said he wasn't working just then, and I got the sense that steady employment had been difficult for him. Ricardo had changed, and it wasn't for the better. The guy I had looked up to so much in high school was no longer cool. I left our meeting feeling very sad.

The tragedy in Ricardo's life was that he was trying to deal with the painful difficulties of his upbringing that weren't his own doing by using drugs. His drug usage helped him cope enough during high school to be one of the most popular kids. But coping with problems isn't the same thing as solving them. Eventually his demons would return, and he needed a bigger and better coping strategy because his old drug wasn't working anymore. A better drug is no solution to emotional pain. Ricardo was turning to a material substance to deal with feelings that could only be dealt with in relationships with other people. Like the rich ruler who was unable to surrender his addiction to his material wealth, Ricardo was in the grips of his addiction to the euphoria that his drugs brought him. Once the euphoria wore off, Ricardo returned to the altar of his addiction for another temporary postponement of his pain. But just as Jesus predicted—idolatry of any kind is very difficult to give up.

Jesus knew that once we come to rely upon material things to make us feel secure, it is very difficult to give them up. This was the point he was making when he said, "It is easier for a camel to go through the eye of a needle than for a rich man to enter into the kingdom of God." Spiritually he wasn't talking about money; he was talking about idolatry. It is easy to become addicted to physical things and believe they can substitute for our spiritual and emotional needs. Once this happens, it is very difficult to walk away.

SPIRITUAL PRINCIPLE: The problem with drugs is that they make you feel better—temporarily.

DRUGS CAN'T HELP YOU GROW

*"Do not work for food that spoils, but for food that endures to
eternal life."*
John 6:27

Ashley is an amazing woman. She has a successful law practice, is
a classical pianist, and is in better physical shape than women who
are years younger. There isn't anything she can't do.

Ashley's goal is to be successful at everything she does, and
most of the time she is exactly that. She came for therapy because
of feelings of anxiety, and she wanted a professional opinion on
how to deal with them.

"Do you do hypnosis?" she asked in our first session.

"No," I replied.

"I thought we might get there faster," she responded.

"Get where?" I asked.

"Get to where I don't feel this anxiety anymore, of course,"
she said in a puzzled tone.

Although Ashley lived a complex life, her approach to therapy
was quite simple: set a goal and get there as quickly as possible.
This strategy had worked well for her in other areas of her life, so
she expected it to apply in therapy as well.

I could see quickly that Ashley and I had competing agendas.
Her agenda was to hire me to help her rid herself of disturbing
emotions. My agenda was to help her understand herself. She was
trying to get rid of her feelings, and I was trying to get her in
touch with them. We had a problem.

Ashley was addicted to success. She needed to be the best,
own the latest, and know the most. She believed that God
wanted her to succeed. The problem was, Ashley had created
God in her own image. What Ashley actually believed in was success and the euphoria her icons of success brought her.

Ashley's worship of success was doing a good job of keeping her from feeling bad about her life. She had everything she wanted. But because Ashley was pursuing "things," the benefit she received from them was limited. If she ever started to feel bad, she would go shopping or plan a trip. If she ever wondered about the meaning of her life, she would think about her career accomplishments. Ashley's success was a great antidote to any painful feeling in her life.

Although Ashley was accomplishing more and more each year, we discovered an interesting thing in our therapy together: she was basically the same person. Her goals were the same, only bigger. Her desires were the same, only less satisfying. On a material level, Ashley was becoming more successful each year, but on a spiritual and emotional level, she was living the same year over and over again. Ashley didn't need a new drug to feel better; she needed a new God.

Ashley and I eventually discovered that her anxiety was telling her something. She was glad that she was successful, but she wasn't really happy. Ashley needed to be giving her life to something that was giving as much back to her. Success is a selfish god—when you worship it, it spiritually depletes you. It will help you collect idols, but it won't help you be a better person. Failure actually does a better job of that. Ashley came to the realization that although her portfolio was growing, she wasn't. She needed to listen to her feelings, not get rid of them.

Ashley is changing gods these days because the last one took more from her personally than she is willing to give now. Her concept of growth is starting to have less to do with the bottom line and more to do with the quality of friends in her life. Ashley isn't in as much of a hurry as she used to be because her new God has a different perspective on time. The funny thing is that even though she isn't accomplishing as many things as she used to, she feels she is living a fuller life.

Jesus was constantly pointing people toward the things that were eternal. He knew our attraction to instant gratification results in temporary satisfaction. He knew that the euphoria of idolatry is only an antidote to the pain and disappointment in our lives. The hurting stops, but only temporarily. This type of antidote neutralizes the symptoms, but it doesn't cure.

Jesus never encouraged people to avoid the suffering in their lives because he wasn't interested in the "quick fix." He didn't want people to feel better; he wanted them to get better. Idolatry not only avoids pain, but growth. While we are preoccupied with idols, we remain immature. Idolatry assists people in avoiding things, while growth only comes from facing them. Whatever our drug of choice is, it will never help us grow.

SPIRITUAL PRINCIPLE: Addicts worship a selfish God.

SEXUAL ADDICTION

*"But I tell you that anyone who looks at a woman lustfully
has already committed adultery with her in his heart."*
Matthew 5:28

Erotic feelings are the normal sexual feelings accompanying the
desire for closeness we feel for someone we love. But eroticized
feelings are the sexual feelings we have for someone that cover
over painful feelings of inadequacy or fear. Erotic feelings tell us
that our relationship is good. Eroticized feelings tell us that
something is wrong, and we want to cover it up with sex. When
we eroticize a relationship, we turn a person into an object and
the relationship into an idol. This can become very addicting.

Luis has never dated much. It's not that he isn't interested in
women; it's just that he never thought they were interested in him.
Luis is shy, not very good at sports, and didn't reach puberty
until later than most of the other kids. He thinks about going out
with women, but his thoughts about that stay mostly in his fantasy world.

Luis has a habit of developing an intense "crush" on a woman
he knows without her ever being aware of it. It usually happens
as a result of some interaction with a female acquaintance at
work. When a woman he finds attractive gives him attention, he
can't help but launch into a fantasy relationship with her. Once
this woman gets into Luis's fantasy world, his thoughts and feelings about her seem to take on a life of their own. Past a certain
point, it's as if he isn't even in control of them.

Although Luis has had several fantasy relationships in his life,
he usually has one at a time. Most people would view him as
obsessed, but Luis thinks of it as falling in love. Because Luis
doesn't believe he has much of a chance for a relationship with
the woman of his dreams in the real world, he turns to his fantasy
world instead. There he can control her reactions to him as well

as his performance with her. In the real world Luis feels like a failure with women; in his fantasies he is a huge success.

Luis is addicted to his sexual fantasies. He returns again and again to them to ward off his feelings of inadequacy. He has done this so often it seems impossible to stop now. Luis is entrenched in a very difficult form of addiction because the "thing" he is addicted to is a fantasy relationship in his mind. This is the problem with sexual addictions: it is difficult to stop being sexual in our minds.

Luis has taken the first step toward creating a more satisfying life for himself—he has admitted that he has a problem. He has come for therapy to try to learn how to be more successful in the real world. Although we talk about sex in our sessions, Luis's problem is not as much sexual as it is spiritual. He is coming to the realization that his addiction to sexual fantasies has enslaved him to a god that takes his time and energy and only leaves him feeling bad about himself. He wants to learn how to relate to people so that he can feel better. Luis's courage to ask for help is the first step toward that goal.

When Jesus spoke about "anyone who looks at a woman lustfully," he was pointing out the dangers of viewing people as sexual objects. He warned against using people like a sexual drug because he knew that anything can be turned into an idol, even our relationships with others. The temptation of sexual addiction can draw us into a fantasy world that may feel good, but never really is.

SPIRITUAL PRINCIPLE: Lust can enhance love, but never replace it.

RELIGIOUS ADDICTION

"Unless your righteousness surpasses that of the Pharisees and teachers of the law, you will certainly not enter the kingdom of heaven."
Matthew 5:20

Ryan attends his church regularly, volunteers for positions of responsibility there, and is always eager to discuss religion with anyone who is willing. Ryan has numerous religious pictures and symbols in his apartment and on his car, but he doesn't believe they are idolatrous. He enjoys quoting the Bible to underscore whatever point he is making, but he is very suspicious of other people who do so if they disagree with his interpretation.

Ryan is very specific about how people should become Christians and what it means for them to live it out. He knows how they should talk, what they should read, what forms of entertainment are acceptable, and how they should think about social issues. Although Ryan claims to have given control of his own life over to God, most people find him very controlling when they are in his presence.

Unfortunately Ryan doesn't want relationships; he wants disciples. He needs to have others affirm his religious convictions by accepting them as their own. He isn't using his religion for the purpose of connection; he is using it for the purpose of imposing conformity. Jesus never intended that.

Ryan has a number of doubts about himself that he can cover over by getting others to admire him for his religious knowledge. He tells them he is only interested in their doctrinal purity, but he is secretly interested in getting them to validate his own perspective. Although Ryan tells people he wants them to follow Jesus, he really wants them to follow him.

Once, one of Ryan's friends suggested that he consult with a therapist because of the difficulty he was having in a relationship with a woman he was interested in. But Ryan is suspicious of psychology. He believes that all problems are the result of a lack of faith and that consulting someone who has studied secular theories couldn't possibly be helpful to him. The truth is, Ryan doesn't want to talk to a therapist because he doesn't want to uncover his doubts, insecurities, and feelings of confusion inside. He likes feeling strong and in control.

What Ryan doesn't realize is that his religion is a form of idolatry because it is being used to cover over painful feelings instead of connecting him to God and others. Instead of understanding his feelings, he covers them over with religious language and rituals. Ryan uses his religion to medicate himself against the pain and suffering in his life, which is the opposite of how Jesus used his. Ryan has become addicted to control, and religion has become his favorite drug to get him there. It will probably take a crisis in his life to get Ryan to reexamine his religion, but then he might be able to choose it again for a new reason: to facilitate his relationship with God.

Jesus saw religion without relationship as idolatry. The Pharisees and teachers of the law were sincerely religious people who didn't think of their religion as idolatrous because they worshiped God. But Jesus warned against using religion to give the appearance of righteousness by hiding our true feelings inside. The righteousness he spoke about would never do that. To him, righteousness based upon relationships surpassed righteousness based upon religious laws. The very same thing Jesus described as religious idolatry, I see in my consultation room as a psychologist today as religious addiction.

The purpose of religion for Jesus was to facilitate a relationship with God and others, not substitute for them. Sometimes people use their religion to make themselves feel better, just as addicts use drugs. In both instances painful feelings are kept hidden behind the use of something tangible. In the case of religious idolatry, the religious laws and rituals become the "drug" giving people the illusion that they are better than they really are. It may appear more socially acceptable, but it is just as addictive.

SPIRITUAL PRINCIPLE: Religion is a path, not a destination.

CAN THERAPY BE AN ADDICTION?

"Trust in God."
John 14:1

Not everyone who comes to therapy really wants to deal with his or her genuine feelings. Some come to therapy to make the painful feelings in their lives simply go away. When people come to therapy with the sole purpose of feeling better, they run the risk of using therapy like an addictive drug. Ironically, it is often those who say they don't want to "become dependent upon therapy" who are most in danger of using it as an addiction. It is the attempt to avoid difficult feelings that leads to addiction, not the genuine expression of them.

Julia was raised in a conservative Midwestern town where she learned the importance of a good work ethic along with traditional religious values. She is conscientious about everything she does and always keeps her word when she makes a commitment. Julia had a terrible relationship with her mother and struggles in her relationship with her husband, but she refuses to blame them for any of the unhappiness in her life. "That's in the past," Julia said when I asked her about her childhood. "I'm responsible for the problems in my life—no one else is to blame."

Julia feels bad about how her life is turning out, but she can't figure out how to change it.

"There's one common denominator in all these bad relationships I've had, you know. Me!" she explained. "I just need to work harder at being a better person."

Ironically, Julia was *too* responsible. What I mean by this is that she blamed herself for everything that was wrong with her life. Julia didn't come to therapy to explore how she felt about things; she believed she already knew. She believed she was at fault, and she just wanted me to tell her how to behave differently so she could make things better. There was a lot Julia needed to understand about herself, but it was hard convincing her of that. For instance, what Julia thought was conscientiousness was actually guilt. She felt guilty about her relationships with her mother and her husband. She felt guilty about many things in her life and blamed herself as an unconscious kind of self-punishment. Unfortunately, Julia was trying to use therapy to avoid these feelings rather than bring them out into the open.

Therapy is most helpful to people when they come for help with the questions about their lives, not when they already have the answers. Julia was convinced that she was her own worst problem, and she believed that raising questions about her feelings or her past was a waste of time. "Fine, so I feel sad about that," she said to me when we uncovered her feelings of grief over her marriage. "So what should I do different?" She had very little interest in her genuine feelings about the events in her life. She was convinced that whatever was wrong was her own fault so it would only make her feel worse to focus on how she felt.

Julia's therapy began to work better for her when she was able to open up to her genuine feelings and trust that the process of doing so would help her grow. She thought talking about feelings was a failure to take responsibility for herself and a failure to trust in how she thought God worked in people's lives. Although she couldn't see it, Julia was trying to use therapy like an addiction. Therapy used to avoid painful feelings doesn't help people to change. And as Julia found out, it doesn't help them to be more trusting in any of their relationships, including the one they have with God.

Julia started to feel differently about her life when she stopped trying to get me to tell her what to do and started trying to find out how she felt about what she had already done. She discovered that her feelings of guilt were causing her to be overly self-critical and began to realize the difference between self-condemnation and personal responsibility. Julia stopped trying to use her therapy to medicate herself against painful feelings and started using it to figure out how to use her feelings in constructive ways in her relationships with others. At first Julia came to therapy because she thought she *needed* it, as if there were something wrong with her that needed medical attention. Over time she came because it was something she *wanted* to do, using it as a resource to help her be the best person she could be. This type of dependence upon her therapy resulted in the strengthening of her relationships with her mother, husband, and God.

Jesus believed we must put our trust in God. To him, God was the ultimate source of strength and power to live life. Some people are critical of therapy because they believe it fosters dependency upon something other than God. Usually, people who believe this either have little experience with therapy or have tried to use it in an addictive manner. I have found the process of personal therapy to be invaluable in helping people uncover their genuine feelings in life and ultimately deepen their genuine trust in God as well as other people.

For Jesus, there was no conflict between trusting God and depending upon others. He depended upon his closest friends and encouraged them to depend upon him in ways that strengthened their trust in God. Our ability to rely upon others by sharing our innermost feelings deepens our capacity for faith.

SPIRITUAL PRINCIPLE: Therapy is a process of healthy dependence.

HAVING NEEDS DOESN'T MAKE YOU NEEDY

"Trust also in me."
John 14:1

"I'd like to work on my self-esteem," Grace announced in our first session. "I know I can be difficult, but most people don't understand me. I hope you can help."

Grace had been in therapy before and believed that she had made a lot of progress, but she was still feeling bad about herself and wanted to work on that. She felt extremely insecure around people and didn't have many friends. She attended a few group meetings at her church, yet never got close to anyone there. Grace saw herself as a kind of misfit who desperately wanted to belong. If people did give her attention, she clung to them as though it were the only bit of human contact she was going to get. Grace hated being such a needy person but couldn't help it.

Grace had been told that she was too dependent upon others and that she should try to be more independent and less needy. She was told that she needed to "get a life" because she had a dependent personality and it was important to "get outside of herself" by focusing on others rather than herself. Grace had tried to develop some interests with a fair amount of success but still felt bad inside.

Initially Grace would call me fairly often between our sessions with some crisis she needed to talk about. We increased the frequency of our sessions, which helped, but Grace still found herself getting into emotional states she just couldn't deal with. She needed to call me to help her through them. Grace hated needing me as much as she did, but she just felt the things she had to deal with were too much for her to handle alone. She didn't want to admit it, but she was afraid she had made an idol out of me and was just too weak of a person to deal with things without me. Grace found herself acting as though she were addicted to our relationship, needing regular "fixes" of me in order to make it through most days.

Over time Grace and I came to see that her problem was not that she was too dependent upon me—it was that she hated herself for depending upon me at all. Grace would try to deal with her emotions during the week when distressing things would happen to her, and she would even tell herself that she wasn't going to call me this time because she needed to handle the issues by herself. This ended up making Grace even more anxious, as she then had to cope with trying not to need me on top of whatever it was that was distressing her in the first place. The resulting increase in her anxiety would make Grace need to talk to me even more, which she would try to fight off, and within a short time Grace would find herself in an unbearable panic. Grace ended up feeling like a drug addict in withdrawal, desperately needing to hear my voice in order to calm down.

Things began to change for Grace when she stopped thinking she was too needy and realized that needing me was a normal part of the process of therapy. Once Grace accepted her dependency upon me, she became more free to deal with her feelings during the week without the threat of shame for needing to talk to me about them. Her phone calls dropped off because she wasn't getting so upset with herself for wanting to call me in the first place. Most of the time, she would simply call my voice mail to listen to my voice and leave a message without needing me to call her back at all. Just knowing that she could depend upon me was enough. Because Grace was not feeling as bad about needing me, she stopped feeling so negative about herself in the process. Perhaps she wasn't a weak person after all, just simply a woman with occasional intense feelings who wanted to know someone else would understand.

Although it took a while, Grace came to understand a fundamental aspect of her humanity that she had been fighting. People are dependent creatures. We need others to be whole. Grace realized in her own life that when Jesus was asking us to trust him, it was not because we are weak and needy, but because it is the only way we can become all we are created to be.

Jesus encouraged people to trust and rely upon him. He did not view dependency as a problem, but as necessary for a fulfilling spiritual life. He understood that humans must depend upon God and each other for survival. To try to be independent was to reject our fundamental nature. To Jesus, it was our ability to be vulnerable and embrace our dependency that led to wholeness. Those who refused to be dependent were only pretending to have everything they needed.

SPIRITUAL PRINCIPLE: Having needs doesn't make you needy.

HOW TO FIND SERENITY

"I stand with the Father, who sent me."
John 8:16

Rudy was addicted to his anger. The endorphin rush that comes with a burst of rage would give him an almost euphoric feeling of power and confidence to deal with the problems in his life. Whenever Rudy felt insecure or threatened, he always had his drug of choice close at hand. He never had to deal with feeling small or weak for very long, because he could turn any situation into one in which he felt big and strong instantly—by getting really mad.

Rudy grew up with a distant father. Probably to compensate for the emotional absence of his dad, his mother was overprotective. Rudy felt insecure on both fronts: he didn't feel as though he measured up to his father's expectations of him, and his mother's overprotectiveness made him feel as if she didn't believe he could do things for himself. He was afraid to try new things even though he was very bright and could figure out how to do them quickly. Rudy hated being afraid, but he couldn't help feeling that way most of the time.

Rudy's boss insisted that he go to therapy because his anger was getting in the way of his performance at work. He didn't like talking about his past with me, and it was hard to identify exactly what he was feeling most of the time. During our sessions I kept trying to get him to tell me how he felt about things until I discovered an important aspect of his personality. Rudy only had two emotions, anger and apathy.

Most of the time Rudy lived with a quiet discontent about his life. He was basically unhappy because he felt as if he were living below his potential. The only time Rudy really felt alive was when he was angry. His anger gave him the ability to focus and feel passionate.

It was easy to see that Rudy's addiction to anger was an attempt to cover over personal feelings of insecurity. He didn't feel good about himself, which made him vulnerable to getting his feelings hurt. This would send him into a rage, and once he got started, it was almost impossible to calm down. Afterwards Rudy would feel worse about himself for losing his temper, which made him even more susceptible to getting his feelings hurt in the future and starting the whole cycle of rage over again.

Over time Rudy and I came to understand that his insecurity came from feeling alone in the world. Since childhood, he had felt his father didn't care about him and his mother didn't trust him. There has never been anyone he could turn to for genuine help. Without anyone to turn to, he felt as though the weight of the world was on his shoulders, and that felt like too big a task for anyone to manage. Who wouldn't be insecure about that?

Gradually Rudy began to let me carry some of his emotional load. As he began to trust me, he found himself feeling less alone and less insecure. His angry outbursts came less frequently because he wasn't getting his feelings hurt as often. And he didn't need to self-medicate with rage. He found that he had a whole range of emotions he could talk about, now that there was someone he could count on to help him sort his feelings out. Rudy needed someone he could stand next to and feel safe. As Rudy let me "stand in" for his parents as someone he could turn to, he discovered an important truth about human nature—a truth that Jesus taught. True serenity comes from knowing there is someone we can rely upon to make us feel safe.

We develop the capacity to soothe ourselves from being soothed by those who care for us. The reason that many people turn to addictions is because they never developed the capacity to self-soothe. They use their addictions to artificially calm themselves down or distract themselves from their fears. Because they never had someone to help them feel safe in the past, they substitute an antidote to their fears to help them cope today.

Jesus knew how to find serenity: stand next to God. All of us are looking for security, and we can only find it by feeling protected from the dangers that exist in life. Where in the universe could anyone find a safer place to stand than next to its creator? Jesus believed that only then could we find true peace of mind. To him, those who find true serenity are never alone.

SPIRITUAL PRINCIPLE: The truly serene are never alone.

YOU CAN'T CURE YOURSELF

"Physician, heal yourself!"
Luke 4:23

The problem with chemical dependency is not *dependency* per se; it's dependency upon a *"chemical."* It is only through dependency upon God and others that we are able to know who we are. Dependency in relationships is a process of mutual interaction that produces growth. Dependency upon a chemical, or a thing, is a one-way process that dead-ends. We must depend upon others to be fully alive. It's dependence upon inanimate objects that leads to spiritual and psychological death.

Douglas had a drinking problem, but he didn't know it. He wouldn't drink every day, but when he did drink he always had enough to numb himself from whatever he was feeling. When I first asked him if he was concerned about his drinking, he quickly said, "No. Are you kidding? I'm having my most successful year ever at work. Sure, I love fine wines with good meals, but I've got nothing in common with those drunks on the street."

Douglas didn't just drink wine with his meals. He would drink after work to ease the stress, he would drink at lunch if he was nervous, and he would drink alone sometimes without knowing why. Most problem drinkers never end up like the drunks on the street, and some of them are actually quite successful at their jobs. However, drinking is a problem if it is used to mask feelings that are needed to have better relationships with others, and that was exactly what was happening with Douglas. He told himself he drank because he liked it, but he really drank because he didn't like how it felt if he didn't. Douglas was drinking to cover over his feelings, which kept everyone at a bit of a distance from him and made it really hard to know what was going on inside.

Although he didn't know it, Douglas's first step in dealing with his addiction was to come for therapy. He needed help expressing his vulnerable feelings, and coming to therapy turned out to be an excellent place for that. It wasn't easy, but Douglas and I did discover emotions buried deep within him that he had been covering up for years. But each week, by the time our next session rolled around, he had successfully covered over his feelings again, and it was as if we were starting therapy all over again. I finally recommended to Douglas that he seek additional help beyond our sessions. I suggested that he go to an AA meeting. In Douglas's case I decided he needed something AA had to offer that I couldn't give him—twenty-four-hour-a-day, seven-day-a-week support. He needed to be a phone call away from help with his feelings whenever he felt tempted to drink them away.

"I don't want to sit around listening to a bunch of losers complain about their lives," he protested. "I've got nothing in common with those people."

"Perhaps," I replied. "But you still need what they've got, and you're not going to find out what I mean unless you go to a few meetings and see for yourself."

Begrudgingly, he went. Over the next several months Douglas discovered some things about himself. He discovered he was drinking to hide from his feelings, especially sadness. He discovered he had never felt connected to other people because he was keeping himself numb when he was around them. Now, even if he was in a room with people from very different walks of life, he discovered a way to have something in common with each of them: he could be honest.

Sometimes Douglas still feels as if he is sitting in a room full of losers when he goes to meetings. But that feeling doesn't last very long because he has discovered another important thing about himself—he needs these people to survive. Douglas now knows he had problems he didn't even realize and he was on the road to increasing isolation back when he was drinking. He says it was just a matter of time before it was going to start affecting his work as well. All that is behind him now, because Douglas has learned how to draw upon a power greater than himself, and as long as he continues to do that he finds healing, one day at a time.

Jesus never believed the spiritual path was something to be traveled alone. He was constantly acknowledging his dependence upon God in everything he did. He recognized that no one could function in isolation, including himself. He did not respond to the crowd's mocking of "Heal thyself," because he did not view himself as ever able to do anything apart from his relationship with God. To him, attempting to heal oneself was a violation of how humans were created to be.

The largest and most popular approach to treating alcoholism in this country has the same view of healing that Jesus did. Step Two of the Twelve Steps of Alcoholics Anonymous is, "We came to believe that a Power greater than ourselves could restore us to sanity." Even though AA does not describe God in the same way Jesus did, it is in agreement that people seeking help for alcoholism must call upon someone greater than themselves. Neither AA nor Jesus would tell people to try to heal themselves.

SPIRITUAL PRINCIPLE: The one who seeks healing seeks another.

LOVE IS THE CURE

"Love each other as I have loved you."
John 15:12

Jordan describes herself as a recovering cocaine addict. "I have two years of sobriety with the program, and I think it's time that I took a look at some of my issues with the help of therapy," she said in our first session.

"I find that personal therapy can be really helpful for people working a program," I assured her. Some people fear that therapists might not be supportive of Twelve Step programs, and I wanted her to know that I was not one of them.

Jordan is an attractive woman who has lived a hard and fast-paced life. Her previous drug use was associated with an extravagant lifestyle that involved wild parties, exotic traveling, and extensive spending. Unfortunately, now she was broke. Grateful for her new life, but broke. "All that fun had a price," she mused, "but I try to be philosophical about it. I guess it took all that to get me where I am today."

Jordan had a long history of intense and superficial relationships with men during her drug days. Now she was trying to figure out how to do things differently. "Things were simpler before," Jordan explained. "I never really expected anything more than a good time from guys, so I never got my heart broken. Now it's all so complicated."

There was really only one feeling that Jordan was looking for when she was using drugs, "getting high." If the people she hung around couldn't understand that, then she didn't hang around them. Jordan wasn't a bad person; she was just very concrete in the way she went about her relationships. She connected through sex and drugs. Those were very real and tangible ways to deal with her relationships.

Jordan is discovering that she has a wealth of other feelings in her life now. She looks back on her drug days with pain and embarrassment over the way she conducted herself in her relationships. She has even gone back to many people and made amends for some of her conduct. She can remember saying "Love you!" to almost everyone she knew then, as if it were a kind of salutation that could instantly connect her to others. She doesn't do that anymore, not because she doesn't love people as much, but because she is starting to find out what it means to love in a much deeper way.

Now Jordan is trying to connect to people using her feelings. She listens to how other people feel and doesn't try to rush them through their sad or unhappy times, because she can tolerate a wider range of feelings than she used to. She doesn't say "Love you!" to people she doesn't know anymore, because she believes knowing them is a part of loving them now. She has male friends because she is learning to love people without the currency of sex or drugs. Her relationships tend to last a lot longer because she is learning to love people for who they are. Jordan remembers what it was like getting high, but isn't interested in going back there because the experience of having mature relationships in which she feels loved is too great a feeling to ever give up. She isn't interested in substitutes for love when she can have the real thing.

Addicts love idols, but idols cannot love back. Addiction prevents love from maturing. When people choose a concrete object as a substitute for love, the development of their maturity is arrested. When the arrested development of addicts is unblocked and growth resumes, they surrender their attachment to idols and seek relationships with others who can love them. Jesus taught that we must love and be loved to mature spiritually, and the idolatry of addiction prevents this from taking place.

Jesus believed love to be the most powerful force in the universe. He taught that God is love, and that love is the creative force to overcome all the problems in the world. Love was central in the teachings of Jesus, and it is the essential element for the healing of the human heart.

SPIRITUAL PRINCIPLE: Love cures.

WHY GOD HATES IDOLATRY

*"Do not store up for yourselves treasures on earth, where moth
and rust destroy."*
Matthew 6:19

To witness the birth of a human being is a powerful event. I never
really understood that until I witnessed the birth of my own son,
Brendan. My wife, Barbara, and I planned for this event for years.
We took an extensive birthing course, became certified in infant
CPR, and read volumes of literature on the subject. We even
made a tape on which I recorded myself reading children's
books, which Barbara played for him when I was at work, so he
could become familiar with my voice while he was still in the
womb. I couldn't have been any more prepared, and yet still I
wasn't ready. Having a child is not something you can learn
about from others; it's something you have to experience yourself to know.

Unfortunately, Barbara's labor was a difficult one. Our obste-
trician was concerned about the baby's size relative to Barbara's,
so she advised us to induce labor a week early hoping for a normal delivery. After thirty-three hours of contractions from one to
three minutes apart, we all came to the conclusion that Brendan's
head was just too large and he was going to have to come into the
world via C-section. The whole experience was grueling, but I
was grateful for the medical knowledge we have now, as I shud-
der to think what might have happened without it.

I will never forget the moment I first saw my son. He didn't
look too bad given what he had just been through, and within
seconds he was trying out his new lungs. "Miracle" is still my
favorite word to describe the experience. Barbara was recovering
from the surgery, so I had the honor of cradling him in my arms
next to her just minutes after the birth. Even though I was
fatigued and somewhat in shock over the gravity of what had just

taken place, I noticed something was happening between Brendan and me almost instantly. As I was trying to pay attention to him, I discovered that he was trying to do the same thing to me. This was not a one-way interaction. We were having the beginnings of a relationship.

When I was in graduate school, the research on infant development suggested that newborn babies couldn't differentiate between themselves and others. Everything was supposed to be an amorphous mass of sensation. These researchers had obviously never held a newborn baby. If I would try to match his breathing, he would respond to mine. If I listened to his noises, he reacted to mine. I think the tape recording we made had an impact upon him, because Brendan actually turned to look in my direction when he first heard the sound of my voice.

I know I can't ask Brendan what he was experiencing during our first encounter in the operating room, but I certainly know the experience I had. I believe I had a glimpse into the image of God on earth. I saw the innate capacity to have a relationship within another human being in someone who was only six minutes old. From our first breath in life we are seeking a relationship with someone outside ourselves. We are born to relate, and this is what is divine about us. Whatever other idols or temptations toward addictions I may struggle with in life, I will never forget how powerful it is to have a loving relationship with my son. This is how we were created to be, and no substitute for this kind of love could ever take its place.

Jesus was familiar with the Old Testament teaching, "You shall not make for yourself an idol in the form of anything in heaven above . . ." (Exod. 20:4). He taught that God was a jealous God, but not in the petty sense of being insecure about losing what he had to someone else. God was protective of the world in the manner in which he had made it and angered by attempts to alter the natural order of the universe as he created it to be.

Jesus taught that the image of God on earth was not a "thing," but the creative capacity for relationship. God is angered by idolatry because it is an attempt to substitute a "thing" for a divine capacity within us. Just as the members of the Trinity are in relationship, God has given us the same capacity to relate to each other and to him. The image of God on earth is therefore not an object, which will eventually decay and be destroyed, but an eternal capacity for relationship that transcends time.

SPIRITUAL PRINCIPLE: To love things is only human; to love others is divine.

PART 2

KNOWING YOURSELF

CHAPTER 7

KNOWING YOUR FEELINGS

At that time the disciples came to Jesus and asked, "Who is the greatest in the kingdom of heaven?"

He called a little child and had him stand among them. And he said: "I tell you the truth, unless you change and become like little children, you will never enter the kingdom of heaven. Therefore, whoever humbles himself like this child is the greatest in the kingdom of heaven.

"And whoever welcomes a little child like this in my name welcomes me. But if anyone causes one of these little ones who believe in me to sin, it would be better for him to have a large millstone hung around his neck and to be drowned in the depths of the sea."

Matthew 18:1–6

Jesus taught that who we are is determined by what we feel in our hearts. He spoke of being born again, living by faith, and having child-like hearts. He wanted us to be childlike because children are innocent, trusting, and open to their emotions. Deeply spiritual people are aware of their emotions.

Jesus loved to challenge the way people think. To be great, he said we must be small. To be leaders, he said we must serve others. To be profound thinkers, he believed we must be able to feel. Jesus taught that the identity of a human being is a matter of the heart. He didn't use the psychological terms we have today to describe emotions, but it is easy to see that Jesus wanted us to be in touch with the way we feel.

Jesus loved, felt anger, experienced fear, cried with sadness, and lived by courage. He knew who he was, and he was motivated by what he felt even if it made no logical sense to anyone else. Our emotions give us the keys to who we are and direct us to do the things we do. Jesus wanted us to know the full range of our emotions.[1]

BE CHILDLIKE, NOT CHILDISH

"Unless you change and become like little children . . ."
Matthew 18:3

Some people are reluctant to be emotional because they believe it is childish. However, there is a difference between being childish and childlike. To be childish is to be immature and refuse to take full responsibility for your actions. To be childlike is to recognize adult responsibilities, yet be able to surrender to emotions. Jesus placed great importance on being childlike.

Being childish requires little effort, but it actually requires strength to open up to our emotions in a childlike manner. Jesus always maintained a mature sense of boundaries and an awareness of the consequences of his actions, yet he had the courage to be vulnerable to his emotions. His childlike openness to what he was feeling made others feel close to him, while his reliable sense of responsibility made them feel safe in his presence.

Harriet had a long history of getting into intense, discordant relationships that never worked out. She had frequent outbursts of anger whenever anyone disappointed her, even though she had had enough therapy to admit that she had issues with abandonment. In her therapy with me, Harriet had a difficult time focusing on what she might be doing to contribute to her relationship problems, but she was very articulate about what other people were culpable for in creating problems for her.

At first, Harriet would often page me after hours with what she considered emotional emergencies. She would be furious with everyone, including me, and felt entitled to express her rage by swearing, screaming, and throwing tantrums. Our sessions were often filled with these types of outbursts. She believed that therapists were supposed to be able to handle these things, as she was desperately trying to get me to understand the depth of her pain.

Her childish outbursts were not helping Harriet in her relationships, and they were not helping her with her own feelings. Harriet was plagued by serious doubts about herself, and she was convinced that other people would not like her if she ever opened up to them. Rather than experience rejection by others, Harriet would act in a hostile manner toward them first. It felt better to be the one doing the rejecting.

As Harriet began to realize how her anticipation of rejection was keeping her from getting what she needed from others, she began to change the way she expressed her feelings. Instead of violent outbursts that created distance, Harriet began to open up childlike feelings of pain and vulnerability that created a connection. What Harriet began to discover for the first time in her life was that if she opened up her emotions in a childlike manner, she became more attractive. Her courageous attempts to be vulnerable made people like her more, rather than less, as she had always feared.

The biggest benefit of Harriet's change in the way she expressed her emotions was the change in how she felt about herself. She stopped automatically fearing rejection by others and began to entertain the notion that who she was inside might not be so bad.

This was the kind of childlikeness that Jesus was talking about. He admonished others to "become like little children" in the ways that made them trusting and vulnerable. Ironically, this is the most powerful way to live.

SPIRITUAL PRINCIPLE: Childish acts alienate, while childlike ones attract.

THE ROLE OF FEELINGS IN GROWTH

"Let the little children come to me."
Luke 18:16

Seven-year-old Brittany was a difficult child. She was frequently angry and aggressive toward others, which made it very difficult for her to get along with other children. She would bite, kick, and scratch anyone who disturbed her, and her temper tantrums were exhausting for everyone, including Brittany. Her parents were alarmed and confused by her behavior, so they sought out professional help. They were afraid that combative children like Brittany ended up relegated to institutions where they were cared for but protected from hurting themselves or others.

When Paula first met Brittany, she knew she had her hands full. Brittany, sitting in the middle of the floor, would be crashing her toys together and generally making a mess of whatever she touched. Asking Brittany why she was being so destructive was useless because she didn't know. She was acting out on the outside feelings she was having on the inside but couldn't express. Once feelings become enacted in this manner they become very difficult to change, because the physical expression of feelings can be very reinforcing.

Paula knew Brittany was trying to communicate emotions that she didn't have the words for. Everyone could see that Brittany was angry, but someone needed to understand that she was afraid. Paula wanted to welcome Brittany's feelings in a manner that made Brittany feel safe. Brittany's violent behavior was an emotional expression that was hurting her in the process. Although no one could control Brittany, she couldn't feel more out of control herself.

Brittany expressed herself physically, so Paula had to meet her there. If Brittany wanted to yell, Paula would say, "Yes, I see how angry you are now." But if Brittany wanted to scratch or bite, Paula would hold her until she could calm down. Because Brittany was both angry *and* afraid, Paula needed to honor both emotions in their relationship. Paula wanted to communicate to Brittany that she wanted to hear all of her emotions, not just the angry ones.

Over time, Brittany has changed as a result of her therapy with Paula. She is still somewhat awkward socially, but she is not as violent as she used to be. She is better able to label her feelings now and so is less in need of acting them out. She has learned that her fear can be expressed and welcomed by others, and this makes her feel safer than she did in the past. Brittany has grown as a person because she can express more of her emotions than she used to. Paula's ability to find the childlike parts of Brittany and pay attention to them is facilitating the formation of a human identity. Their relationship is an example of the growth that can take place when we welcome all of the emotions that someone brings to us, just as Jesus did.

Jesus always welcomed children. He knew the importance of being responsive to childlike openness. We now know that the human brain needs to experience responsiveness to feelings in order to develop properly.[2]

Each time a child is able to identify a feeling, such as "I'm sad" or "I'm happy," the child develops a stronger sense of who the "I" is that is having the feeling. The child learns that "I" am the one having the sad or happy feeling as opposed to it coming from someone or somewhere else. Parents who pay attention to their children's feelings are actually helping their children solidify an identity that will carry with them throughout life. Helping children—and adults for that matter—identify their feelings helps them grow.

Jesus' eagerness to welcome children is a psychological model for us. In welcoming the emotional spontaneity of children, he was encouraging their growth. His responsiveness became the hallmark of his healing presence, which was felt by all who encountered him.

SPIRITUAL PRINCIPLE: A child's identity is formed in the heart more than in the head.

THE ROLE OF FEELINGS IN OUR CONNECTION
TO OTHERS

"Happy are those whose hearts are pure, for they shall see
God."
Matthew 5:8 (Living Bible)

Jesus taught that spiritual people relate heart to heart. Emotional understanding creates a bond. We feel approval when others agree with us intellectually and we are comforted when they physically protect us, but we only feel connected to them through shared emotional experiences. The pure in heart have a special connection to God not just because of their guilelessness, but because of their ability to know clearly how they feel.

Saundra and Ben came for marriage counseling with one of the most common afflictions I see in marriages today: poor emotional communication. Both were professional people with successful careers before they got married. When they began their family, they mutually decided that Saundra would stay at home full-time to care for the children. They were happy with this arrangement, satisfied with the amount of money that Ben brought in for the family, and pleased with how their children were doing. What they couldn't stand any longer was the constant fighting between them.

Saundra and Ben couldn't solve their arguments because they didn't understand the importance of emotions. Both Saundra and Ben thought they should be able to negotiate the disagreements in their relationship following the same rules they had both successfully used in their respective business careers. Unfortunately, the rules at work are not the same as the rules at home. Coming to an agreement on what they should do is irrelevant if they feel terrible about each other once they have reached it. *How* marriage partners talk to each other is just as important as *what* they talk about.

Saundra would try to bring up a concern she was having about one of their children. Ben would tell her what he thought they should do about it. Saundra would feel dismissed by this quick response from Ben reminding her of how insignificant she felt growing up, and as a result she would typically disagree. This would make Ben defensive, reminding him of the constant criticism he got growing up under his father's perfectionism, and he would argue his position even more strongly. These conversations would almost always end the same way. One of the two would throw up his or her hands in disgust, blurt out, "Fine! Then just do it your way!" and stomp out of the room. A decision would be made, but a marriage was being lost in the process.

Eventually Saundra and Ben came to realize that making decisions while losing the connection between them was no way to live. Being intimate with your associates at work is not important; being intimate with your spouse is. This is why the rules at work won't work at home. The social contract is different. The goal at work is to get things done. The goal at home is to get things done while loving each other. Paying attention to feelings is how you do that.

Saundra and Ben are feeling better about their marriage these days because they recognize that the emotions accompanying each of their conversations are just as important as the content. Ben doesn't rush to fix problems quite as quickly as he used to because he realizes the pressure to perform comes more from his childhood than his wife. Saundra checks herself before she automatically disagrees because she doesn't feel the need to prove herself any more. Now when Saundra starts to feel dismissed by Ben, she can tell him how it feels and that she is reminded of earlier feelings. And Ben is able to say that he feels bad when she feels that way because he isn't trying to dismiss her. He just is eager to help and sometimes a bit too enthusiastic with his answers because of the pressure he felt from his dad. Saundra and Ben have learned an important truth about connection between people; that is, intimacy is experienced through the clear expression of feelings. Their inability to know clearly how they felt was the result of previous emotional experiences for both of them that happened long before they were married. They were not able to experience intimacy without a greater clarity of heart. As Jesus predicted many years ago, a happy relationship is a matter of being pure at heart.

If others disagree with what we think, we can dismiss them. But if they invalidate our feelings, we can be deeply hurt. Jesus never placed intellectual correctness above purity of heart. He knew that people connect through emotions, and that our most serious disagreements are not over what we think, but the result of how we have been emotionally hurt.

SPIRITUAL PRINCIPLE: The rules at work don't always work at home.

THE SECRET TO SURVIVING SUFFERING

"Do not let your hearts be troubled. Trust in God; trust also in me."
Jesus taught that the key to surviving suffering was to remain connected to God. If we allow God to remain with us in our suffering, no matter how bad it feels, we can mature through the difficult times. Anything is tolerable if we do not have to endure it alone.

"Do not let your hearts be troubled. Trust in God; trust also in me."
John 14:1

Jesus taught that the key to surviving suffering was to remain connected to God. If we allow God to remain with us in our suffering, no matter how bad it feels, we can mature through the difficult times. Anything is tolerable if we do not have to endure it alone.

Rick was one of the shortest kids in his class growing up. He was always the last one chosen to be on a team, and the bigger kids often picked on him. Rick tried to avoid situations where the other children might have an opportunity to tease him for being so short, but it happened frequently anyway.

Rick didn't end up bitter about being short, in part because of his relationship with Greg. Sometimes kids form a special friendship that lasts throughout life. Rick and Greg had that kind of friendship.

One time it was pretty embarrassing for Rick, because Greg was with him when one big bully stuffed him in a trash can just for fun. Without saying a word, Greg just gave Rick a knowing look as if to say, "Yeah, I know. That guy is a real jerk." That was what Rick needed, one other person to be there for him. It was as if they were both being teased, and somehow that made it less painful.

Rick would never want to relive his childhood, but he doesn't spend much time feeling resentful about it either. It felt awful being the shortest kid around, but most of the time it was tolerable because he always knew Greg would understand how he felt. His life is better today because he had someone to share his feelings with during the difficult times. This is the secret to surviving suffering that Jesus wanted us to understand.

Some of the wisest people I know have suffered a great deal in life, but so have some of the most bitter people I know. Jesus knew that suffering could make us either better or bitter. His own suffering was an inevitable part of his life, and facing that suffering well was central to his mission on earth.

Jesus demonstrated how to survive suffering as an example for everyone. He didn't write a book about suffering or hold a series of lectures on the subject, but he did model it for us. Even in his most difficult times, Jesus never lost his connection to God. He didn't try to go through suffering alone. He didn't want us to try to do that either.

SPIRITUAL PRINCIPLE: Suffering is tolerable if we do not have to tolerate it alone.

WHY SUFFERING TURNS TRAUMATIC

"If the demon leaves . . . it returns and finds the man's heart
clean but empty! Then the demon finds seven other spirits
more evil than itself, and all enter the man and live in him.
And so he is worse off than before."
Matthew 12:43 (Living Bible)

Some children who have had to suffer very difficult circumstances turn out relatively normal, while other children who have
gone through much less suffering seem more psychologically
damaged. The explanation lies in the difference between psychological injury and psychological trauma.

Psychological injury is the damage sustained when we are
emotionally hurt. This happens to all of us. Our caregivers might
fail to provide for our needs in some significant way, or we might
be exposed to some overwhelming circumstances or attacked by
someone in a way that is emotionally wounding. Life is dangerous, and people get hurt.

Psychological trauma results when no one is there to support
us and help us make sense out of our injuries. Then psychological injuries can turn into events that become proof that we are
weak, incompetent, defective, or maybe just cursed. A hurtful
event becomes traumatic when it takes on a negative meaning
about who we are. Traumatic past events can become demons
that haunt us for a lifetime. Having someone there to respond to
our pain makes all the difference. Jesus knew that we need help
from others when we have been injured to keep the demons from
returning to hurt us even more.

Candice is an attractive and intelligent woman. Although you
might not be able to tell it by looking at her, Candice has had a
life-altering experience. When she was a teenager she was raped
while walking home from a friend's house one night. It was the

most horrifying event of her life. She would erase it from her memory if she could.

Before Candice came to therapy, she had never spoken about the rape in detail. She told her parents what happened that night, they filed a police report, and that was the end of it. She didn't want to go to the rape counselor the police suggested, and her parents thought that talking about it would only further humiliate her and never brought it up again.

Candice has difficulty in her intimate relationships with men because of the rape. She doesn't want it to affect her, but it does. She tenses up at the thought of being sexual with a man and finds herself fearful around strong or assertive men. Candice didn't know it, but it is not good to keep certain secrets to oneself.

Candice fell into the trap that many rape survivors fall into. She couldn't help thinking, "If only I had asked for a ride home that night," "That dress I was wearing drew too much attention," or "How could I have been so stupid?" Candice was blaming herself. Blaming the victim is something we do to try to make sense out of random acts of senseless violence. But in Candice's case, it turned her injury into a lasting trauma.

Perhaps if she had been able to talk to someone, her secret might not have been so damaging. Someone else could have helped her see that her feelings were not abnormal and she did nothing to cause the event. The event was a bad thing, but she was not bad for having it happen to her. If Candice had not been left alone to deal with her feelings, this horrible event might not have turned into such an ongoing trauma that made her feel bad about herself almost daily. Demons love to work in secret, but they run away when they are forced out into the light.

Candice is starting to feel less fearful around men because she is working on her feelings in therapy. She needed to talk about what happened to her and to share her feelings. Closing the door on her past injuries did not keep the demons out, but letting her therapist into places that were dark and hidden is sending them away.

Jesus knew we all have to suffer injuries, but we don't have to live our lives traumatized because of them. He believed that if we share the burden of our injuries with someone we trust, it can help prevent the injury from turning into a trauma. Time alone doesn't heal. If we don't seek help, the demons from the past can return.

SPIRITUAL PRINCIPLE: Time alone doesn't heal.

HUMAN BEINGS ARE RATIONALIZING ANIMALS

"For a man's heart determines his speech."
Matthew 12:34 (Living Bible)

Christopher believes that emotions are a sign of weakness. His mother struggled with depression when he was a child, and his father would often discipline him in rage. He vowed he would never be like them. Christopher's wife divorced him after four years of marriage because "she wasn't getting her emotional needs met," which only further convinced him that people who live their lives by their emotions end up destroying everything around them.

Christopher knows that the vast majority of divorces are initiated by women who base their decision on their emotions. He believes the evidence is clear. Rational people can be trusted, and emotional people are weak and pathetic. His only mistake in his marriage was in not recognizing how emotional his wife was before he married her.

What Christopher doesn't realize is that his conclusion about emotions predates any evidence he has collected about marriages over the years. The hurt Christopher feels over his childhood is still locked away. Because of that, he wasn't able to be emotionally intimate with his wife, which caused the marriage to end long before she left him. His insistence that her being "overemotional" was the cause of the divorce was really a rationalization he used to protect himself from ever being emotionally vulnerable. He was too afraid to risk getting hurt by his wife after all the hurt he had endured because of his parents. It wasn't that his wife was too emotional; it was that he was not emotional enough.

Christopher has a rational argument for how emotions have wrecked his life. What he doesn't see is the role he has played in the destruction. Christopher's decision to avoid emotions was itself an emotional decision—he only convinced himself that it was a rational conclusion. Unfortunately, because Christopher had rationalized his feelings away, the belief that emotions are destructive became a self-fulfilling prophecy in his life.

Advertising agencies, politicians, salespeople—anyone who deals with how we make decisions knows that impulses, desires, and feelings are the real motivations behind our decision-making process. We often pretend we are objective and rational, as if to lend a kind of credibility to our conclusions. The truth is, we follow our hearts to the conclusions we come to even if we insist otherwise. We then find the logic to support our decisions later.

Humans are not rational animals—we are rationalizing ones. Jesus himself often followed the passion of his heart even when it made no logical sense to those around him. He knew that in the end we all make the most important decisions in life based upon how we feel in our hearts.

SPIRITUAL PRINCIPLE: We justify in our minds what we decide in our hearts.

THE LIMITS OF LOGIC

*"For the Kingdom of God belongs to men who have hearts as
trusting as these little children's."*
Luke 18:17 (Living Bible)

Diane called me for marriage counseling because of the constant
bickering between her and her husband, Chuck. I was impressed
with how intelligent they both were in our first session, and I
could only imagine how convoluted and heated their arguments
must become because each had the ability to be articulate in making a case or defending a position.

Diane started a particular grievance with, "I want to talk about
Tuesday when you were yelling at me and out of control."

Chuck jumped in with, "Why won't you stick to the facts? We
agreed to work on the taxes together on Tuesday, and you failed
to keep our agreement!"

"And it was also our agreement that I would handle the
arrangements for your company party this weekend, which was
exactly what I was doing at the time," she countered.

Often, they would both have good points, and I would sometimes get lost in the details as they each presented their side of the
argument so logically.

Sometimes a keen intelligence is both a blessing and a curse.
Logical people are often organized and efficient, but that same
logic can make them approach relationships with a mechanical
precision that can get in the way. Chuck's and Diane's logical reasons for being angry with each other weren't helping their marriage. Finding feelings of compassion for each other's distress
might.

Things changed when Chuck and Diane stopped giving logical reasons for why they were so angry and started opening up
to the childlike feelings of vulnerability that gave rise to their
anger.

"I got mad because I often feel insignificant to you. On Tuesday I felt like what I wanted just didn't matter to you," Chuck shared.

"Insignificant?" Diane replied. "I never thought you felt that way. I thought you were mad at me for disappointing you. Nothing is more important to me than you. I'm sorry you felt that way."

Chuck and Diane were learning that logic has a limited role in solving their arguments. They needed emotional vulnerability to get to the solutions they both desperately needed.

Our lives would be very difficult without the benefits of our rational capacities. However, when it comes to our relationships with other people, logic is limited in helping us achieve what we need.

Jesus didn't talk about the Kingdom of God as if it were a physical location; he spoke about it as if it were a direction of the heart, something that we enter into with our hearts through a trusting relationship with God. We can use reason to approach God, but we can only enter into a relationship with him by the faith we have in our hearts. To Jesus, logic can get us only so far in life. At some point we have to trust by the faith in our hearts to go the rest of the way.

Jesus never said that being logical was wrong; it's just that it is secondary in healing our pain. To get to the deepest parts of our relationships, we must lay down our logic when it has taken us as far as it can and trust the feelings in our hearts to guide us the rest of the way.

SPIRITUAL PRINCIPLE: The heart can lay hold of things that cannot be grasped in the head.

WHY WE DO WHAT WE DO

*"Do not be afraid of those who kill the body but cannot kill
the soul."*
Matthew 10:28 (Living Bible)

Charles started his first session with, "My wife thinks I work too much and that I have a problem with anger." Sometimes men come for therapy because their wives think they need it. It usually takes a while for these men to come to the realization themselves that they need therapy.

Charles assured me that he knew he wasn't perfect but that he didn't really need therapy. He insisted that he worked as hard as he did because it was necessary to pay the bills and that he only got angry when the situation called for it.

"I'm only doing what's natural," he would insist. "Only the strong survive out there, you know." Charles was a believer in natural selection, so he admired aggressiveness and despised passivity. He was convinced that he was only following his nature by working as hard as he did and that having an "edge" was something that he needed to be successful. If his wife couldn't understand that, then she just didn't have a grasp of how the world really works.

As our sessions progressed, I began to see that Charles had reasons for being the way he was that didn't have anything to do with being "natural." Although he didn't like talking about the past, Charles described his relationship with his father as a bad one. His father was a rigid taskmaster who liberally exercised corporal punishment. Charles can never remember him saying the words "I love you."

Charles worked as hard, and as angrily, as he did because he was trying to prove something. He was trying to prove that he wasn't weak and that he did amount to something, as if someday he could stand up to his father and say, "So there!" Of course, Charles would never admit that his father still had that much influence over him. Eventually he came to see that just because he refused to mention his father's name didn't mean his father had stopped impacting his life.

Charles was not motivated to be the way he was simply because of some natural instinct men have to get to the top of the pile. He was motivated by how he felt about himself because of his relationship with his father. He wasn't as angry as he was simply because of an excess of testosterone; he was mad about being made to feel small, and he wasn't over it yet.

When Charles began to realize that certain feelings were motivating him, things began to change. He still wanted to be successful, but he began to think about success less in terms of winning and more in terms of being good at what he does. He started to realize that he could be strong without having to be angry. *How* he advanced in his career was just as important as whether he was advancing. Charles thinks more about how he feels these days, because he has come to realize that his feelings play a big role in motivating him to do the things he does, and they always have.

According to Jesus, human emotions are more complicated than the instincts that motivate other animals, like the ones that motivate birds to fly south for the winter. As humans we don't procreate based solely upon instinctual drives; we make love. We don't merely evolve through self-preservation; the more evolved humans can lay down their lives for their friends. There is something very extraordinary about the human heart.

Jesus taught that as people we are special not just because of our intelligence or opposing thumbs, but because of our ability to feel deeply about things in our souls. He told us to "not be afraid of those who kill the body but cannot kill the soul" because our biology did not determine who we were as much as our souls. The heart is the seat of human motivation, because our feelings are the real basis for what we do.

SPIRITUAL PRINCIPLE: Feelings are the energy that drives the human soul.

EMOTIONAL INTELLIGENCE

*"Otherwise they might see with their eyes, hear with their
ears, understand with their hearts."*
Matthew 13:15

Laura and James were ready to divorce. Unfortunately, many
couples let their relationship get to this point before they are willing to come for marital counseling. This was the second marriage
for both of them, and they were horrified to find themselves on
the brink again.

They were both angry, and they were both convinced that
their anger toward the other was justified. She was hurt by his
emotional unavailability and he by her constant criticism of him.
They had both come to the conclusion that they wanted out, and
coming to therapy was simply a last-ditch effort.

After a few weeks of refereeing, putting out fires, and calling
fouls, our sessions settled down to a level where both Laura and
James could admit an important truth to each other. Neither of
them actually wanted a divorce—they each thought that was
what the other wanted, and neither wanted to be the one being
left.

What they wanted was for things to change. Laura didn't want
James to go away; she wanted him to be closer. James didn't want
a life without Laura; he wanted her to be happy with him. They
were about to make a terrible mistake because they were not considering all of the information they needed to make their decision
about a divorce. Their real feelings for each other needed to be
considered. The problem was that they were just covered over by
pain and disappointing circumstances.

Laura and James are still having problems, but things are
somewhat better now. They have agreed to keep working on the
issues they don't like about their relationship, but with one
important difference: they have agreed to stop threatening each

other with a divorce. As difficult as it is, both Laura and James can find the feelings of longing underneath the feelings of hurt and anger that give them what they need to make the best decision about their marriage. Listening to *all* of their feelings, even the hidden ones, is turning out to be the most intelligent thing to do.

Psychologists are discovering that people are successful in life because of the effective use of their emotions as well as their intellect. Daniel Goleman calls this "emotional intelligence."[3] The truly powerful life makes intelligent use of feelings as well as facts. Rather than leading us astray, as some people think, our emotions are an important source of information necessary for a full comprehension of things. Without input from our emotions, we end up making decisions without all the data—not a very smart thing to do.

When Jesus decided to seek out a group of disciples for his inner circle of friends, he did not make education or even intelligence his first criterion. He selected those who could "understand with their hearts." He didn't try to change the world with a new philosophy or a better set of spiritual principles that could be taught academically. He knew that the Kingdom of God would be spread by the impact of what people felt in their hearts. Jesus understood the power of emotional intelligence.

SPIRITUAL PRINCIPLE: The best decisions are made with all the available data—from both the head and the heart.

CHAPTER 8

KNOWING YOUR UNCONSCIOUS

"The knowledge of the secrets of the kingdom of heaven has been given to you, but not to them. Whoever has will be given more, and he will have an abundance. Whoever does not have, even what he has will be taken from him. This is why I speak to them in parables: 'Though seeing, they do not see; though hearing, they do not hear or understand.' In them is fulfilled the prophecy of Isaiah: 'You will be ever hearing but never understanding; you will be ever seeing but never perceiving.'"

Matthew 13:11–14

We can be looking right at people and not see them, or listening to people speak but not hear them. Jesus knew that forces outside of our conscious awareness operate in our minds, often preventing us from dealing with the things that are right in front of us. He understood that aspect of the human mind we now refer to as the unconscious.

The unconscious is a way of describing how our minds filter our thinking. It is our minds' way of keeping us from thinking about everything all at once. Because we can't deal with everything all at once, we can't be fully aware of *all* that is going on in our own minds at any point in time. The fact that our minds operate unconsciously is not a problem; being unaware of it is.

We work on our unfinished business in the unconscious. Troublesome or undone things from the past are often revisited in the unconscious. In fact, we will go over them again and again until something changes. Without realizing it, we keep repeating the past in attempts to get it right. This is why it is important to know your unconscious. Without that awareness, "you will be ever hearing but never understanding," because some very important things you need to understand are hidden in your unconscious.[1]

PEOPLE LIVE BY FAITH, NOT BY SIGHT

"We live by faith, not by sight."
2 Corinthians 5:7

Jesus knew that what people think in their heads is not nearly as powerful as what they believe in their hearts. Sometimes what we are certain are facts are really beliefs that we have unconsciously convinced ourselves are true.

Joseph Breuer was a nineteenth-century physician who was fascinated with symptoms such as "glove hysteria," which is the numbing of the hand from the wrist to the fingers as if the patient were wearing a glove of numbness. The interesting thing about "glove hysteria" to Breuer was that it was neurologically impossible based upon his understanding of human anatomy, yet it was a symptom reported by certain of his patients. These patients were *certain* their hands were physically numb even though Breuer knew this could not be the case.

Breuer came to discover that his patients who felt guilty about what they had been doing with their "numb" hands, or what they fantasized about doing with them, were cured from their "glove hysteria" through the process of talking about their repressed fantasies and sexual feelings. During the puritanical times in which they were living, these kinds of explicit conversations about sexuality were discouraged, and consequently rare. This process of bringing unconscious thoughts and feelings into conscious awareness, which led to the cure of these patients, he termed the "talking cure."

Breuer's work with his patients became more complicated as they began to develop sexual feelings toward him that were rooted in unconscious thoughts and feelings from their pasts. These patients became *certain* that they were in love with Breuer. This "transference" of feelings from his patients' unconscious onto him made him uncomfortable, so he turned the major part of his research into the unconscious over to his younger associate who was much more comfortable dealing with the people's beliefs and fantasies, Sigmund Freud. The rest is history.

In societies with a general awareness of the unconscious we rarely see symptoms like "glove hysteria" anymore. We understand that "Freudian slips," dreams, and sexual feelings all have unconscious meaning, which we can talk about more openly now. Because we are better able to make unconscious beliefs conscious, they do not have the control over us they used to. Things we were *certain* were true can be transformed into beliefs we only *thought* were true.

Jesus was making a spiritual statement about belief in God when he said, "We live by faith," but perhaps he was also making a psychological statement about how people live their lives. Confronting people who are rigidly clinging to their beliefs with facts won't change their minds because they have come to their conclusions by "faith, not by sight." But if their unconscious beliefs can be made conscious, they aren't experienced in the same way anymore. Once we realize what we thought was factual is actually a matter of belief, there is room for change. Facts can't change, but beliefs can.

SPIRITUAL PRINCIPLE: We see what we believe.

WE ARE CREATURES OF HABIT

". . . holding on to the traditions of men."
Mark 7:8

Miguel agreed to come for marital counseling with Adrienne after years of pleading on her part. Adrienne's complaint was that Miguel was too demanding and critical. Miguel didn't think they needed counseling, but he was willing to come to appease her. They both viewed their marriage as a "traditional" one, because Miguel was the sole source of income and Adrienne had elected to stay at home with the children. This arrangement was fine with Adrienne, but she had grown dissatisfied with Miguel's controlling attitude toward her and the children. It seemed Miguel was convinced that they should live out the traditions he grew up with, but Adrienne was experiencing the way he was going about that as authoritarian and demeaning.

"My parents have been together for fifty years, which is more than I can say for most people," Miguel proclaimed. "What's wrong with trying to follow their example?"

"You're forgetting what it was like when you lived at home, Miguel," Adrienne responded. "Everything is not so perfect in your family."

After a few sessions, Miguel did come to admit that although he respected his father, he only reached that point after a few years of rebelling against his dominance in the family. "Sure, he was hard on me. But that was the only way I was going to learn," he insisted. Miguel's father believed in corporal punishment and frequently spanked him with a belt. The unfortunate consequence of this for Miguel was that it left him with an unconscious conclusion about a father's authority: for a man to be respected in his home, he must be feared by all who live there.

Miguel was trying to follow his father's authoritarian example without remembering that he hated living under it himself. Without realizing it, Miguel had come to fear losing the respect of his wife and his children unless he maintained a dominant stance with them. Unconsciously, respect and fear had become confused as the same thing. This made him believe that he needed to dominate the members of his household or he would be a failure as a husband and father.

Miguel is starting to realize that the traditions he was trying to follow were rooted in unconscious beliefs about himself. He can now see that this left Adrienne in the awkward position of having to deal with Miguel's absolute certainty about how their family should be run without much room for her perspective. This was exacting an unnecessary price on their marriage. Miguel is no longer living out his role as a father and husband based upon his fear, and Adrienne is finally coming to feel that her opinion does really count. Miguel needed to come to the awareness that following traditions unconsciously can be dangerous. Becoming aware that he was in the grips of beliefs that were outside of his conscious awareness is helping him do that.

We are creatures of habit. We find security in our routines and identity in our traditions. Some habits are good, and Jesus recommended that we follow certain traditions to help us relate better to each other and to God. He knew that sometimes we need something tangible to make the love in our relationships feel real.

The problem comes when we engage in habits unconsciously. This causes us to repeat activities from our past without being fully aware of why. Jesus didn't want people to follow habits and traditions without being aware of why they were doing so. Following traditions can be good, but following them unconsciously may not be.

Jesus warned us about holding on to traditions, not because they are bad, but because we often hold on to them unconsciously. The question isn't *whether* or not we have family traditions; it's *why* we do. If our traditions enrich our families, then they are a good thing. If they don't, then we need to heed Jesus' warning.

SPIRITUAL PRINCIPLE: Habits based upon fear defile traditions based upon respect.

DON'T BE SO CERTAIN OF YOURSELF

"But your guilt remains because you claim to know what you
are doing."
John 9:41 *(Living Bible)*

Unconscious thoughts are experienced as absolute facts. This means we don't *think* we know something unconsciously; we are *certain* that is true. When we're living our lives based on unconscious thoughts and feelings, we think we know what we're doing, but the truth is we're not fully aware of why we are doing it at all. Jesus never asked people to be perfectly certain of themselves; he asked them to be self-reflective.

I met Tommy in a home for boys because he was a ward of the state. Even though he was only seventeen, he had some definite ideas about life. He trusted no one and didn't expect anything from anyone. He would steal if he could get away with it, lie straight to your face, and never display a hint of remorse when he got caught. Tommy thought he was pretty smart, and he was certain that everyone else was stupid.

There was no convincing Tommy that his perspective was skewed. He had been taken away from his mother at a very early age, and he never knew his father. Being bounced around through several foster homes had made his early life very unstable and left him with the conviction that nothing is certain in life and no one can be trusted. "No matter what people say, they're only in it for themselves," Tommy said. "People are worthless." This was his motto.

Tommy was a hard guy to help. He wasn't interested in help. He was absolutely certain that he was right in his assessment of people and had no interest in anybody's ideas to the contrary. To trust others was to be a "sucker," and if he could take from others it just proved that he was smarter.

What Tommy couldn't realize was that he was in the grips of unconscious beliefs. He unconsciously believed *he* was worthless, which was what made him so angry and reckless. Because he had never been cared for in the way that he needed, he had come to the unconscious conclusion that he didn't deserve it. But because this was an unconscious belief, he experienced it as a fact. If you are *certain* that you are worthless, then you don't have anything to lose. He didn't believe anything could help, and he wanted to keep people at a distance to avoid the pain of being seen for what he thought he was.

Unfortunately, people who have unconscious negative ideas about themselves don't see those ideas as beliefs; they just think those ideas reflect "just the way they are." In cases such as Tommy's, the results can be quite devastating. He spent his life engaging in self-destructive behavior and going nowhere. Things only began to change when Tommy began to realize that it wasn't his belief that other people were worthless that caused him to act the way he did. He was battling his unconscious belief that he was the one who had no worth. Ironically, as we started to confront his unconscious conviction that he was worthless, he became less certain that other people were that way as well.

People like Tommy act as if they are absolutely certain they are right. Jesus often challenged those with this kind of rigid thinking to be more flexible. He knew that if people are too rigid in their thinking, they are often guilty of missing something important. Sometimes they miss important truths about others—but often also about themselves. These are the people whose "guilt remains" even though they are absolutely certain that they know what they are doing.

SPIRITUAL PRINCIPLE: If you rigidly think you are right, think again.

BUT WE'VE ALWAYS DONE IT THAT WAY!

*"And why do you break the command of God for the sake of
your tradition?"*
Matthew 15:3

Dirk's father was a successful, hardworking contractor who gave
everything his best effort and demanded the same from Dirk.
Dirk admired his father, so he played football in high school like
his father did, married a woman a lot like his mother, and went
into the construction business just like his dad. Dirk's father was
hard on him and even threatened to "break his neck" if he didn't
follow orders. Dirk tried to keep from displeasing his father
whenever he could.

Dirk lived a very physical life. He worked out at the gym to
develop a massive physical appearance and sometimes got into
fistfights with other men at the local bar. Dirk knew his father
hated weakness, and he wasn't about to back down from anything or anyone.

One day Dirk took his family to the county fair. He was trying
his luck at the carnival shooting range when he noticed another
man looking at him out of the corner of his eye. Dirk stopped and
suddenly turned to face the man, preparing for a confrontation.
At *exactly* the same moment the other man turned to face Dirk.
Dirk was frightened by the massive arms on the man, and the
stern, intimidating look on his face caused Dirk to take a step
back. Then he realized he was looking into a glass mirror next to
the shooting range. Dirk had frightened himself.

Dirk learned something about himself that day. He was walking around trying to frighten and intimidate others because he
was unconsciously trying to cover over his own fears of not measuring up to his father's expectations. He was living out the life
that his father had taught him because it was familiar, not because
it was truly satisfying.

People choose the familiar even if it's not good for them. They sometimes cling to old patterns for unconscious reasons, reasons that actually get in the way of making things better. Jesus challenged others to examine their traditions and ask themselves if they really wanted to keep living their lives in the same patterns.

Jesus said, "A new command I give you: Love one another" (John 13:34). The command of God is to love; the demand of the unconscious is to follow the familiar. Sometimes the two are in conflict with each other. The test for our traditions should be whether or not they help us love God and others. If they don't, then we need to look for unconscious reasons that trap us in the traditions we hold so dear.

SPIRITUAL PRINCIPLE: Choose love over familiarity.

CURE IS FROM THE INSIDE OUT

"First cleanse the inside of the cup, and then the whole cup
will be clean."
Matthew 23:26 *(Living Bible)*

Marty suffers from panic attacks. During a bad one, Marty thinks she is having a heart attack and is going to die. Her heart races, she can't breathe, she breaks out into a sweat, and her knees get weak, making her think she is going to faint.

Marty tries to control her panic attacks, but it doesn't do any good. On her way to my office she will tell herself that she isn't going to let it happen this time. But inevitably she will get caught at a red light, trapped in a lane that has no exit, or perhaps cut off by another driver. Any of these things will bring up an anxious feeling for Marty, and then she is in trouble. As soon as Marty feels anxious, she tries to rid herself of her anxiety, which only makes her more anxious. This makes her feel as if she is going to have a panic attack, which of course makes her even more anxious. Her attempts to control this level of anxiety usually result in a system overload, or a panic attack. Her very attempt to control her panic attacks causes them.

Marty's problem was that she was trying to fix her problem from the "outside in." In other words, she focused on her behavior, not her beliefs. Trying to control her behavior (her anxiety) only confirmed her beliefs (anxiety is dangerous). Marty started to receive help when she realized that cure is from the "inside out." Marty had to first realize that she unconsciously believed that all anxiety is dangerous and causes panic attacks. Once this notion became conscious, she was open to the possibility that this was only a *belief* and did not have to be the case. The next time something happened to make her anxious, she had a better chance of not feeling she had to control her anxiety. This allowed for the possibility that she could be anxious like everyone else.

She learned that without making it worse by trying to control it, the anxiety can pass.

At the deepest level, we all live by beliefs we hold in our unconscious. These beliefs guide our behavior automatically without our even thinking about it. When these beliefs are negative or self-condemning, then our behavior is often self-destructive. Becoming aware of these unconscious beliefs is the only way to effectively change our external behavior in a way that will last.

Jesus knew that the only way to change people's behavior permanently on the outside was to change what they believed on the inside. Unless we are able to get to the deep places within ourselves, we are destined to live lives influenced by the residue of the past. Changing our external appearance or even committing ourselves to new behavior is not likely to last unless we uncover the motives that lie deep within. This is why Jesus told us to cleanse the inside of the cup first.

SPIRITUAL PRINCIPLE: Lasting change is from the inside out.

WHAT YOU DON'T KNOW CAN HURT YOU

*"Every kingdom divided against itself will be ruined, and
every city or household divided against itself will not stand."*
Matthew 12:25

Darlene came for therapy to work on her relationships with men.
She longed to find the right man to settle down with and eventually have children, but even though she was in her mid-thirties
she had yet to become romantically involved with any man.

"My biggest problem," she confessed to me, "is that I believe
I am ugly."

I was somewhat surprised to hear this from Darlene, since I
found her to be attractive and she was always attentive to her
appearance and conduct with others. Darlene went on to
describe her painful self-consciousness around men and the awkward feelings she dealt with every time she thought about getting
involved with a man romantically.

"I know I'm not stupid, and I can be interesting to talk to at
times. But I can't stop thinking that any man I might be interested in would find me physically repulsive. I'm sure there might
be some guy who might want to have sex with me, but I don't
think anyone I would find attractive would *really* feel the same
way about me."

Darlene grew up with an angry father who made life difficult
for her. She never knew what to expect when she would come
home from school, because she never knew if her father was
going to embarrass her. He was usually loud and abusive toward
her and her mother when he had been drinking, which made
Darlene often wish that she were invisible. She would have traded
lives with anyone on the planet if she could have.

Unfortunately, Darlene's mother was of little help to her. She
was passive and unable to control her husband or protect Darlene
from his outbursts. Darlene was left to vacillate between hoping

that someday her father would see how good she was and stop abusing her and at other times wishing he were dead. Neither of these hopes left Darlene feeling very good about herself. Eventually, Darlene developed the belief that her father must not see anything in her that was worth changing his behavior for; that and the awful way she felt about him made her feel like an ugly person inside.

Darlene was locked in a conflict between her unconscious beliefs about herself and her conscious daily life with others. Unconsciously, she believed she was an ugly person who wasn't worth much even though consciously she knew her life was different now. It was only when she became aware of her unconscious belief that she was ugly, formed through her father's abuse, that Darlene started to identify the battle between her conscious and unconscious. She was still angry for the way he treated her as a child, but she could start to believe that she wasn't necessarily an ugly person for feeling this way.

We are continually transferring our unconscious beliefs based upon past experiences onto the world around us today, constantly viewing the present through the unconscious grid of our past. We usually don't know we are doing this, because we do it automatically. The only way we can make room for genuinely new experiences is to become aware of how we are superimposing these old beliefs upon our world today.

This creates a conflict for us at times. Our present-day reality tells us one thing, but our unconscious beliefs tell us something else. Unfortunately, the unconscious usually wins out. This is often the source of the psychological problems in our lives, which can have damaging consequences. Just because we don't consciously know something doesn't mean it can't hurt us.

Jesus called us to greater awareness. That awareness was the key to resolving a "household divided against itself." If we believe something unconsciously that is in conflict with what we think consciously, then we enter into a battle with ourselves and become "divided." What we don't know can hurt us, especially if it is in our own unconscious. Jesus wants us to find freedom from the things that keep us from being consciously aware.

SPIRITUAL PRINCIPLE: You can't win a fight with yourself.

MEMORY IS NOT REALITY

"Come, follow me."
Matthew 4:19

Eunice and Joe came for marriage counseling after forty-five years of marriage. All their children were grown, and Joe had recently retired from his job. This left them with lots of time to spend with each other. As sometimes happens in this kind of situation, they needed help in making the transition to a new stage in life.

One of the difficulties I faced in my work with Eunice and Joe was the fact that they had been carrying on firmly entrenched arguments for years. Heated debates would arise instantly between them based upon circumstances that were decades old.

"It was in the blue Chevy when we were living in Kansas City," Joe would start out.

"No! We were in the green Ford, and we were still in Chicago," Eunice would counter. And so on, and so on . . .

They were both operating on the assumption that if the other person would simply agree with the facts of the matter as they saw it, their arguments would come to an end.

"I said I would be home at eight fifteen," Joe would yell.

"You distinctly said SEVEN O'CLOCK!" Eunice would follow with, as if in the same breath.

What Eunice and Joe finally came to see was that reconstructing history as precisely as possible was never going to solve their disputes with each other. In fact, this was an impossible task after all these years. Their arguments began to finally resolve themselves when they each realized that the facts of the matter weren't as injurious as what those facts *meant* to each person.

When Joe was late again, Eunice was able to say, "Well, I was frightened that something had happened to you. I don't want to be a lonely old lady so soon."

Then Joe could respond with, "I had no idea my being late scared you. I thought you were just mad at me for getting forgetful. I feel bad that you sit home afraid."

Figuring out who had the best memory started to become less important. When Eunice and Joe began to realize that memory is not reality, they started to listen to each other in much more helpful ways.

Unlike many religious leaders throughout history, Jesus never wrote anything down, and establishing a set of spiritual laws by which people should live was never a primary goal. He seemed to know the psychological principle we understand today—that no matter what he said, people were going to remember it through the grid of their own unconscious beliefs anyway. He didn't see the truth as something we could memorize or intellectually grasp. He saw it as something we continue to discover daily.

Jesus knew that he wasn't going to really change people's lives by trying to get them to remember what he said. He knew they would have to live it. This is why he said "Follow me" instead of "Follow my spiritual principles." Psychologists know that trying to get people to remember something in exact detail is next to impossible. As a friend of mine who's a marketing expert is fond of saying, "Perception is reality." This isn't a philosophical statement; it's a practical one. People can only remember things from their own perspective. We must rely upon people more than memory if we expect to do well in our relationships.

SPIRITUAL PRINCIPLE: Don't confuse memory with reality.

HEALING HATRED

*"Why worry about a speck in the eye of a brother when you
have a board in your own?"*
Matthew 7:3 (Living Bible)

We hate in others what we cannot stand in ourselves. One of the
questions I get asked from time to time is, "How can I know
what I have in my unconscious that might be hurting me?" To
answer this, I tell people to think about all the things they dislike
in other people. Then I tell them to make a list of the top five
things they hate the most in others. It is likely that they have
these five things buried somewhere deep in what Jungian analysts
call the "shadow side" of their unconscious.

Bill is so vehement about his hatred of the immorality in the
movie industry that no one ever initiates a conversation with him
on the subject. They already know where he stands. To Bill, sexual purity has become the evidence of true spirituality in our
time, and Hollywood has declared its abdication to evil for not
recognizing this fact. He describes actors who perform in sexu-
ally provocative movies as "immoral" or "twisted" and insists
that they lack character because they have allowed themselves to
be filmed around people who are not fully clothed.

Susan, his thirteen-year-old daughter, is afraid to discuss her
desire to go to the movies for fear that she too will become the
object of Bill's wrath. Like most of the kids her age, Susan
admires many actors and doesn't find their movies as objection-
able as her father does.

Bill thinks the people who make movies with sexual content
are just trying to control others through their sexual feelings and
that anyone who pays to see these movies is succumbing to evil
desires. Susan wants to feel as normal as her friends, about both
her sexual feelings and her desire to go to the movies. What Bill
can't see is that his condemning attitude toward sex in the movies

isn't just toward graphic displays of gratuitous sex; it is also toward the people in the movie industry themselves. This has caused Susan to be afraid to talk about her own feelings for fear of being condemned too. Unfortunately, Bill and Susan are growing farther and farther apart as father and daughter at exactly the time in Susan's life when she needs her father to be accessible to her. Susan would like to talk to her father about sexual matters, but she just doesn't dare.

Bill can't see how his hatred toward actors he believes are trying to control others through sex is actually a way of being controlling himself. He secretly struggles with sexual fantasies on a regular basis and hates himself for giving in to them. Over the years Bill has concluded that the only way for him to control his attraction to pornography is to hate the lustful feelings stimulated in him by it. He feels so controlled by his sexual feelings on the inside that he desperately tries to control everyone else's on the outside. There are two tragic problems with Bill's approach to sexual feelings: it doesn't work; and it is driving an impenetrable wedge between him and his daughter. Bill needs to stop focusing so much on his condemnation of sex in the movie industry and start focusing more on his condemnation of himself for his own sexual feelings.

Jesus seemed to understand that when we find ourselves hating something in others, we would do well to consider if we have something like that in ourselves. Condemning others for a particular fault that we struggle with ourselves is like worrying about a "speck" in someone else's eye that we can do nothing about while we have a "board" in our own eye that is in need of immediate attention. Sometimes the healing of our hatred toward others begins with an honest examination of what we hold in the unconscious parts of ourselves.

SPIRITUAL PRINCIPLE: The hatred of others is often the symptom of an inner wound in ourselves.

HISTORY REPEATS ITSELF, UNLESS . . .

"How can anyone enter a strong man's house and carry off
his possessions unless he first ties up the strong man?"
Matthew 12:29

When I went into therapy myself for the first time, I knew my central issue was my relationship with my father. I was constantly in conflict with him and resentful of how he had treated me growing up. I rarely had contact with him as an adult and had come to shorten my visits home during holidays to avoid ending up in one of our typical meaningless fights.

I remember one session in which I was explaining to my therapist how miserable my childhood was. "It was a 'kick the dog' syndrome," I explained. "He would have a rough day at work and come home and take it out on us. Because I was the most verbal one in the family, it would only take a few minutes before he was yelling at me for something."

To drive my point home I recounted the time when I was eighteen and had secretly timed my father's tirade over the length of my hair. "I knew I was in for a bad one that day, so I looked down at my watch. Two and a half hours later he was still screaming at me and I hadn't even said a word yet. Can you believe it? Two hours of yelling without any provocation from me at all!" I'll never forget what my therapist said next.

"He must have loved you very much."

"What?" I gasped.

"Sure," he continued. "Why else would he have put out all that energy trying to correct you? At your age, he could have simply thrown you out of his house. I don't think he was fighting *with* you; he was fighting *for* you the best way he knew how."

I had never thought about it that way before. I remember feeling as if my therapist had come into one of the darkest closets in my psychological house and wrestled a monster to the floor that

I couldn't handle by myself. I had only one way of looking at my father's anger up until that moment, which was to assume that he was disgusted with me. Perhaps he could have been angry with me because he wanted my life to go better. In his own way he might have been trying to get me to look at things he thought were important.

I was repeating my history with my father every time I saw him because I was interpreting his anger in exactly the same way. Because of my therapist, a window of opportunity was opened that helped break the cycle. I was still tempted to get into the same old arguments when I saw my father after that, but it wasn't quite the same. Because I was more aware of the unconscious way I was interpreting his anger as rejection of me, I started to see that I might be able to interpret it as something else. Our relationship wasn't magically healed, but it wasn't exactly the same after that either.

Jesus knew that we don't *have* to be doomed to repeat history, but history will repeat itself unless we get help from others. When we only see things from our own perspective, we need the perspectives of others in order to truly understand ourselves. Then we can choose to live new and different lives because we are more aware of the unconscious influences on our minds.

The spiritual mission that guided the life of Jesus resulted in psychological benefits for everyone who came in contact with him. Today we call that psychotherapy. In the life of Jesus, it was simply the way he was. People become aware of their unconscious through the aid of another person. Sometimes the "strong man" we need someone else to help us tie up is the unconscious part of ourselves.

SPIRITUAL PRINCIPLE: History doesn't change; perspectives do.

CHAPTER 9

KNOWING WHOLENESS

To some who were confident of their own righteousness and
looked down on everybody else, Jesus told this parable: "Two
men went up to the temple to pray, one a Pharisee and the
other a tax collector. The Pharisee stood up and prayed about
himself: 'God, I thank you that I am not like other men—rob-
bers, evildoers, adulterers—or even like this tax collector. I fast
twice a week and give a tenth of all I get.'

"But the tax collector stood at a distance. He would not
even look up to heaven, but beat his breast and said, 'God, have
mercy on me, a sinner.'

"I tell you that this man, rather than the other, went home
justified before God. For everyone who exalts himself will be
humbled, and he who humbles himself will be exalted."

Luke 18:9–14

Jesus was critical of self-righteousness because he believed that dependence upon God, not self-sufficiency, was the key to wholeness. It
requires humility to recognize that we are not God and know that we
are in need of a relationship with him to be spiritually whole. That
same humility allows us to understand that we also need each other to
be emotionally whole. We lose our humility and pretend to be superior
to others when we are afraid to admit that we need them.

The current trend in psychology also recognizes the importance of
our dependence upon others. The outdated notions of the "Me generation" and "Looking out for number one" are falling by the wayside as
we are finding that humans have a fundamental need to relate to someone outside of themselves. We are not self-contained units, but inter-
connected relational beings.[1]

The common starting point for both spiritual and psychological wholeness is our need for a relationship with something greater than ourselves. Healthy dependence in relationships produces healthy people. Needing others makes us stronger, not needy. Jesus' followers were never to think of themselves as better than other people because they needed those very people in order to be whole. Unlike the Pharisee, we need to thank God that we *are* like other men and women, for that puts us on the path to knowing wholeness.

THE WAR BETWEEN PSYCHOLOGY AND
RELIGION

*"To some who were confident of their own righteousness and
looked down on everybody else . . ."*
Luke 18:9

Over the years I have had a number of religious patients come to
me for psychotherapy. In certain cases I needed to be very careful because of their prejudice against psychology, but eventually I
discovered some helpful approaches. Wanting to share what I
learned with other professionals, I wrote an article and submitted
it to a prominent professional journal for psychotherapists.

To my dismay, the article was rejected. The editor of the journal included the comments by the reviewer in his rejection letter
to me. I was surprised by the reviewer's comments, which were
terse, hostile, and very derogatory. By the end of his review,
which passionately argued that the subject matter had no place in
a psychological journal, he was typing in incomplete sentences
because he was so angry. It was clear to me that he never finished
reading the article because several of his objections were
answered in the latter part of what I'd written.

I had written the article to help psychotherapists understand
the prejudices of religious patients. However, a number of psychotherapists are also in need of help with their prejudices against
religion. The narcissistic need to look down on others we do not
understand is the self-righteousness that injures our own spiritual
and psychological health. Having my article rejected by that journal is ironic in view of the point of the article: whether we are
dogmatic about religion or psychology, the decision to view ourselves as superior to others and not in need of what they have to
offer only results in doing damage to ourselves. Eventually my
article was published in a psychological journal known for its
interest in both psychology and religion. However, I couldn't

help thinking that the readers of the first journal may be the ones most in need of what I was trying to say.

What Jesus criticized as self-righteousness is called narcissism in psychological terms: when one's grandiose view of oneself is used to defend against imperfections, which then becomes an impediment to relationships with others. False-self grandiosity is the barrier to both spiritual and psychological health.

Some people do not believe psychology and religion are compatible, going so far as to describe the antipathy between them as a "war." If there is a war between psychology and religion, then it is the result of false-self grandiosity. When psychology is too narcissistic to admit that religion has anything to offer in the understanding of human behavior, then it is guilty of self-righteousness. When religion is too self-righteous to admit that psychology has anything to offer in the understanding of the human heart and mind, then it is guilty of narcissism. Those who are humble enough to admit that they can learn from others without looking down on them are on the path of psychological and spiritual health that Jesus talked about.

SPIRITUAL PRINCIPLE: The arrogance to believe we are more than others comes from the fear that we are less.

WHEN RELIGION IS A DEFENSE

"God, I thank you that I am not like other men."
Luke 18:11

"God fulfills all my needs," Taylor proclaimed in her first session with me. Theologically I understood what she meant, but I was uncomfortable with the way she said it. I was getting the impression that Taylor had only come to see me because her pastor had told her to, not because she really believed she needed therapy. Her marriage was falling apart and she needed help, but even her pastor couldn't get through her platitudes in a way that was genuinely helpful.

Taylor was convinced that her husband was failing in his spiritual role in their marriage. "His disobedience is leaving us open to Satan," she insisted. Taylor believed she was submitting to her role as a spiritual wife, and she bitterly resented her husband's failure to fulfill his role as the head of their household. The traditional roles Taylor and her husband had chosen for their marriage were not the problem. It was the way that Taylor was going about living out her role that was causing the distress to her marriage. She claimed that she needed her husband to fulfill his obligations in the marriage, but she was living out her obligations without needing anything emotionally from him. She thought she should only be dependent upon God to meet her needs, but she still blamed her husband for her unhappiness.

What Taylor didn't realize was that she was using the language of her religion to avoid feeling dependent upon her husband. She had a long history of being disappointed by important people in her life, and her solution was to never allow herself to be dependent upon another human being again. She wanted to believe that she could be perfectly happy only depending upon God. What she couldn't bring herself to accept was that the only way to be truly satisfied in an intimate relationship would be to allow herself to be dependent upon her imperfect husband to meet her emotional needs as well.

Because it was frightening to depend upon her husband to meet her emotional needs and the risk of disappointment was too great, Taylor placed her focus on the roles and rules in their marriage. The result of this strategy was that Taylor eventually felt superior to her husband in her knowledge of their religion, but increasingly dissatisfied with their marriage. Correcting her husband's religious imperfections was never going to make Taylor happy. Depending upon him emotionally, although this was a dangerous thing for her to do, might. Jesus never intended religion to be used as a defense to make ourselves feel spiritually superior to others. He meant it to be used as a vehicle to create greater intimacy with God. When used correctly, it can have the same effect on our relationships with other people as well.

Sometimes people use religion to cover over painful feelings of inadequacy so they can convince themselves that they are not "as bad as others are." Pretending that they "are not like other men" gives them the illusion that they can achieve spiritual maturity based upon their own superior efforts. In this case, religion is being used as a defense against the fact that we are dependent upon our relationship with God, and others, for our own wholeness.

Jesus leveled his harshest criticisms against religious people. He believed religion to be a helpful vehicle to assist people in their quest for a relationship with God. When he saw religion used in the service of anything else, it grieved him and made him angry. Religion can be used as a defense, but when it is, it fails to be the religion Jesus practiced.

SPIRITUAL PRINCIPLE: Recognizing our commonness makes us special.

WHEN PSYCHOLOGY IS A DEFENSE

*"Whoever does not believe stands condemned already because
he has not believed."*
John 3:18

Madison is well on her way to a successful career in advertising.
She owns her own home and is making use of the compound
interest in her retirement account, which will make her very comfortable in her old age.

Madison is very up-to-date in her appearance as well as her
thinking. She wears the latest styles and reads all the latest books.
Madison has been to see a psychotherapist, but only briefly,
because she believes she has really gotten more out of the weekend seminars that she attends on self-development. She believes
one should never focus on the past, never give in to feelings, and
always emphasize the positive. Madison believes the greatest love
of all is the love you have for yourself, because you can't love anyone else unless you love yourself first.

Madison makes decisions quickly, but she comes off as somewhat cold. Her business opponents fear her, but so do the men
she dates. She complains that men can't deal with her independence, when it is actually her fear of dependence that is driving
them away. The men she dates are not as afraid of her intelligence
and competence as they are of not being needed. Madison uses
what she has learned from psychology to cover over any feelings
of dependence she might have on a man. This façade of invulner-
ability makes her more effective in the adversarial business environment, but less effective in the world of personal love. Madison
is having a hard time accepting that the rules of war and love are
not the same. Unfortunately, Madison is using psychology to
protect herself from her relationships when it would be best used
to do the opposite—make her more vulnerable and connected.
Madison is using psychology as a defense against dependency,

and this will never help her get what she needs from her relationships with men.

People like Madison believe they should be able to love themselves without having to have anyone else to do it for them. They say that ultimately we are alone in the universe and only weak people refuse to accept this fact. Although these people claim to have great faith in themselves, Jesus referred to them as unbelievers because they didn't believe in anything greater than themselves. They "condemn" themselves because of their lack of faith in God and other people.

Jesus taught that human beings must trust God in order to be whole. This is difficult for many people to accept. To avoid dealing with their need for a relationship with someone other than themselves, they use psychology to convince themselves that all they really need is the self-sufficiency to do things for themselves.

SPIRITUAL PRINCIPLE: Strong defenses win wars but lose loves.

JESUS PREACHED RELATIONSHIPS, NOT RULES

"By this all men will know that you are my disciples, if you love one another."
John 13:35

Jack came to therapy because he made an agreement with himself that if he lost his temper and broke something one more time, he would seek professional help. Jack always tries to keep his word. Jack doesn't really believe he has a problem with anger; he just thinks that most people are too lax in their behavior, and he finds this very irritating. He always tries to do the right thing. Why shouldn't he expect the same from everyone else? Jack feels entitled to get angry when others let him down.

The difficulty Jack had with therapy at first was that he couldn't figure out the rules. He wanted to know how we were supposed to start the sessions—whether we were supposed to pick up where we left off last time—and exactly what types of things we were supposed to be talking about. Jack believed that the good people in life follow the rules and the bad people screw it up for the rest of us. This is why he tried to follow the rules in all aspects of his life, religiously.

It took Jack a while to grasp it, but good therapy, like good religion, only uses rules to facilitate better relationships. There is no value in following the rules for their own sake. It is only when they serve to make our relationships better that they are fulfilling their purpose. The reason people were frustrating Jack to the point of anger was that Jack saw keeping the rules as the most important indicator of being a good person. He didn't like the thought that a good person might have to sacrifice some rules at times in order to preserve his or her relationships with others. Jack had been making rules more important than relationships, and that doesn't work very well when people are involved.

Jack started to realize that he did have a problem with anger when he perceived that our sessions together had more to do with our relationship than with the rules of therapy. He became angry with me for not living up to what he thought the rules should be, but came to the conclusion that there was something helpful about being understood by me even if I didn't seem to perfectly meet his expectations with regard to the rules. Jack started to believe that I was important to him because of who I was rather than because of my ability to perform to his expectations. It was only then that Jack realized that this is exactly what he wanted to feel for himself. He had been following the rules so religiously because he was afraid that he could never be thought of as a good person if he didn't. Jack is starting to believe that it doesn't have to be that way anymore. He is starting to believe that others might find him valuable for who he is even if he doesn't perform to their expectations. Jack is beginning to understand the difference between his religion, in which rules are preeminent, and the religion of Jesus, in which relationships are.

Jesus didn't preach a philosophy of life, and he didn't leave a set of religious rules to be followed. He spoke in analogies, offered spiritual principles, and talked about love as the hallmark of those who followed him. He said, "By this all men will know that you are my disciples, if you love one another," because that was the purest explanation of the religion he preached. His was a religion of relationship, not rules.

Psychology is coming to the conclusion that human beings cannot exist apart from a relationship with someone other than themselves as well. We are recognizing that relationships are the atmosphere we need in order to survive. Infants who are not held fail to thrive, life-long partners die within months of each other, and loneliness is the greatest cause of suicide. The religion of Jesus was relationship, not rules, because that is what we need to survive.

SPIRITUAL PRINCIPLE: Loving relationships are the evidence of true religion.

ENCOURAGEMENT

"I tell you that this man . . . went home justified before God."
Luke 18:14

According to Jesus, God does not require us to change before he can love us; it is because he loves us that he encourages us to change. It is in those quiet moments when we long to be better people and admit to ourselves that we are far from perfect that the feeling of being loved by God encourages us to grow. Encouragement motivates us toward wholeness.

At first, I thought my therapy with Jessica was off to a good start because of the positive attachment that she appeared to have to me. "You seem to really know what you are doing," she said. "I guess I'm really lucky to find someone as good at his job as I am at mine." But as time went on, it became apparent that her idealizing comments about me were having an ironic impact upon her. Instead of feeling better in my presence, she seemed to feel worse. Even though she believed I was a great therapist, she seemed to feel bad because of it.

"It was really smart of you to become a psychologist, because I'm sure you don't have to put up with the kind of frustrations in your job that I do with mine," she would complain. "I mean, they are all basically idiots. I'm probably the smartest person in the office, and nobody seems to appreciate it." Jessica seemed almost embarrassed that her life wasn't going as well as she imagined mine to be.

I eventually came to realize that each time Jessica looked across the room at what she believed to be a successful person, it made her painfully aware of how she felt privately about herself—like a failure. Although she would frequently reassure me that she was doing very well in life and that her difficulties at work were the result of the personal problems of the people around her, the truth was Jessica didn't feel very good about who she was inside. Jessica was secretly discouraged and didn't want anyone to know about it.

What Jessica needed wasn't a therapist who had it all together—it was one who would be interested in her if she didn't. Jessica didn't need to talk about how ideal either she or I were; she needed a safe enough place to talk about how she longed to be better than she felt she was. Once Jessica began to talk about her self-doubts and how she wanted the appreciation of others but feared she wouldn't get it, our therapy took on a different quality. Instead of conversations focusing on her idealized abilities, or mine, we began discussing more genuine unmet longings for acceptance.

Paradoxically, something happened in our relationship that Jessica had never imagined. Instead of feeling worse about herself for talking about her inadequacies, she actually started feeling better. Trying to get attention by focusing on having it all together was actually discouraging Jessica, but sharing her longings to grow and improve was starting to make her feel encouraged. Jessica was learning that it was more important for her to receive encouragement from others than to try to impress them. This was an important step in understanding what she needed for wholeness.

Jesus taught that we have a God who is intimately interested in everything about us not because he waits to judge us for wrongdoing, but because he cares about how we are doing. We matter to God. When we admit our most confidential thoughts and feelings to him, he accepts us for who we are. This is a profound source of encouragement.

Jesus taught that we have an ontological need to be growing and that we need the encouragement of God in order to keep doing it. Anyone who has raised a child knows about this basic human need. Whether it's stacking blocks or pursuing the Nobel Peace Prize, we need our efforts to matter to someone else. We need encouragement to grow.

SPIRITUAL PRINCIPLE: Don't change to be loved; grow because you are.

SECURITY

"Father, into your hands I commit my spirit."
Luke 23:46

Nicholas is an anxious man. He suffers from panic attacks that make him feel as if he is going to have a heart attack. Embarrassed about his condition, Nicholas is often afraid to go anywhere or do anything that might cause him to run the risk of having another panic attack.

Nicholas remembers his childhood as being very difficult. He did not really have anyone to whom he could turn for support. Nicholas was afraid of his father, and his mother seemed too busy with the other children to pay much attention to his concerns. Whenever Nicholas was afraid, he would have to come up with strategies to deal with his fears on his own.

If children grow up without anyone to calm them down when they are afraid, they don't develop the ability to self-soothe. Nicholas has a problem with anxiety today because he never learned in his childhood that he could be anxious or afraid at times and that these feelings were only temporary and could be made to go away. Nicholas longed for someone to look up to who would make him feel safe when he was afraid or anxious. Because he didn't get that, Nicholas has a difficult time feeling secure when he becomes anxious or afraid.

Nicholas is having fewer panic attacks today because of the help he is receiving from his psychotherapy. Nicholas is learning to trust in someone who will help him when he needs it. He looks up to his therapist because he believes he is knowledgeable and powerful enough to help him. He is starting to be able to calm himself down because he believes there is someone else who can help him when he can't do it for himself. For the first time in his life Nicholas is starting to feel secure. His therapy is a concrete example on an emotional level of what Jesus was displaying spiritually when he whispered, "Father, into your hands I commit my spirit," as he faced death.

Human beings have a fundamental need for security. We cannot develop into healthy adults without it. Children who were raised in homes where they didn't feel protected often grow up to have emotional problems. And adults who live with insecure feelings about their future suffer from excessive anxiety. We need to have a relationship with someone ideal enough to make us feel safe.

One of the most comforting things Jesus had to say was that the same God who was powerful enough to create the entire universe was personal enough to take our private concerns seriously one at a time. It is a secure feeling to believe that one is in the hands of an omnipotent God. Jesus was able to do everything he did because of it.

SPIRITUAL PRINCIPLE: No one falls out of the hand of God.

YOU ARE NOT ALONE

*"For where two or three come together in my name, there am
I with them."*
Matthew 18:20

Austin is a bright, energetic graduate student who plans to
become a psychologist. He decided that the only way he could
become an excellent therapist would be to go through the process of therapy himself (a belief that I strongly hold too). I started
seeing Austin in psychotherapy several years ago, and I have been
impressed with the growth and changes he has undergone in his
life.

At first, Austin needed encouragement from me because he
was insecure about himself as a beginning therapist in a number
of areas. My willingness to listen without judgment to his fears
and foibles as he was getting started in his career was crucial to
the success of our therapy in the beginning. Then he needed the
security of a relationship with an older therapist who could help
him remain calm as he developed through his stages of growth.
Knowing he had a safe place to process his personal responses to
his patients and colleagues helped him remain calm in the face of
difficult situations. Eventually, Austin came to the point where
what he needed from me was to feel a kindred spirit between us.
He needed to feel that there was someone else in the world who
was *like* him. He needed to feel that there was someone who
loved the same work he did, felt similar feelings, and looked at life
in pretty much the same way. Austin knew we were two different
people, but two people who were very much alike in important
ways. Our therapy sessions became a source of community for
Austin, one that helped him launch his life's work in a healthy
and grounded way.

Toward the end of our therapy together, I became as much a
mentor to Austin as I was his therapist. A mutual respect developed

that empowered him to seek out other relationships with colleagues in which he could give and receive a sense of professional community. Our professional relationship as patient and doctor ended as it should have, but Austin's need to feel that he was not alone continued on.

We need to feel that we are not alone and that there are other people who are the same as we are. No one wants to feel strange. We need to know that someone else can identify with us, that someone else will "know what we mean." Beyond feeling *understood* by others, we need to feel that there are other people who are *like us* in important ways.

Jesus understood the human need for community. We need each other in order to feel whole. Jesus taught that spiritual people are one with each other in a mysterious way. There are no "Lone Rangers" when it comes to spiritual wholeness. When we live in true spiritual community, we can feel the presence of God connecting us to each other.

Jesus was addressing an important psychological need of his followers when he told them to "come together in my name." They could look around the room and see a group of people looking quite different from each other but having something profoundly in common at the same time. We need to know there are other people like us. To be whole, we need to know we are not alone.

SPIRITUAL PRINCIPLE: No person is complete without a kindred spirit.

BEING LOVED FOR WHO YOU ARE

"And even the very hairs of your head are all numbered."
Matthew 10:30

It was a good thing that Mary and Daniel came for marriage counseling. Mary loved Daniel, but she found living with him very stressful. Daniel was a man of high moral principles who was committed to his religious beliefs and valued his reputation in the community. Mary was a free spirit who valued being responsive and open to others. Daniel was a "black-and-white" kind of guy, while Mary lived mostly in the "gray areas." They both had a lot to learn from each other, but they each found the other quite frustrating.

Daniel believed strongly in right and wrong. Mary believed in considering the other person's feelings first. In many situations it would have been difficult to say which strategy was the best one to take. Sometimes Daniel was the more prudent one, and sometimes Mary was the more loving. The difficulty was that, for Daniel and Mary, their differences meant disagreements. This was a problem in their marriage.

Daniel believed that a man and wife should become "as one flesh" and that they should be in agreement and of one mind in their decisions. Mary didn't always feel the same way about things. Daniel experienced Mary's different opinions as a defiant opposition of him. Mary felt Daniel was too judgmental.

Although Mary respected Daniel for his integrity and faithfulness, she still wanted him to change. Daniel loved Mary for her compassion and insightfulness, but he thought her refusal to pay attention to detail was a character defect. Both Mary and Daniel didn't like having a spouse so different from themselves. They each thought intimacy meant agreement, so they questioned their marriage based upon the fact that their personalities were different. Both Mary and Daniel thought they had made a mistake by getting married, and neither knew what to do about it.

Although it was somewhat harder for Daniel, they started to argue less when Daniel and Mary shifted their perspective on the differences between them. Being different didn't have to mean something was wrong—it could also be a sign of strength in their marriage. Daniel learned why "A cord of three strands is not quickly broken" (Eccl. 4:12) when he started seeing how their differences could work together to make a union stronger. He began to see that a bond formed through love was always more powerful than one based on conformity. The spiritual and psychological wholeness of Daniel and Mary's marriage improved once they were able to apply this lesson to themselves. As Daniel and Mary appreciated their differences, instead of resenting them, they did continue to disagree about things, but these disagreements resulted in fewer arguments.

Jesus taught that each person's distinctiveness as an individual is so important to God that he knows the number of "even the very hairs of your head." Jesus did not believe that humans should be isolated individuals, but he did see us as having unique characteristics that we bring to our relationships with others. Our distinct personalities must be appreciated if our relationships are to be whole.

This paradox is difficult for some to grasp. They think that if we are all a part of the same community, then we cannot be different in any way—we must walk, talk, dress, act, and smell alike in order to be a part of the same group. Jesus did not agree. He believed that the strongest relationships allow for individual differences between people. Our ability to tolerate these differences is a sign of spiritual and emotional health. To be in a relationship does not mean we have to be the same. In fact, the most mature relationships take delight in the fact that we are not.

SPIRITUAL PRINCIPLE: Differences do not have to mean disagreements.

THE MISSION OF JESUS AND PSYCHOLOGY

"For God loved the world so much that he gave his only Son so that anyone who believes in him shall not perish but have eternal life."
John 3:16 (Living Bible)

Zachary came to therapy because he wanted to figure out why his relationships with women always ended so badly. It turned out that his biggest problem was really something else. Zachary had a big problem in the area of intimacy with his mom.

Zachary was angry with his mother. She never showed an interest in the things he did when he was in school and was constantly critical of him while he was growing up. He never remembers hearing the words "I love you" coming from his mother's lips. Zachary feels ripped off when he thinks about what a lousy mother he had. The last conversation he had with his mother ended just like most of them—in disappointment. He had had it. Zachary didn't want anything more to do with her.

"What's the point?" he grumbled. "She's never been interested in me, so why should I keep trying to get blood out of a turnip?"

The problem Zachary had with his mother was being transferred onto his relationships with the women in his life. It didn't take long for it to get transferred onto me in our therapy. If I were a minute late for our session, it would infuriate Zachary, or if I talked too much or too little, he would become annoyed.

"Look, this is my time!" he would insist sharply. "I expect to get your full attention for what I'm paying."

It didn't take much on my part to make Zachary think that I was as disinterested in him as his mother was. I could see why there were problems in his relationships with women.

It took a long time before Zachary and I could talk about his broken relationship with his mother. We had to work through all the breaches in our relationship first. Each time I did something that communicated to him that he was unimportant, we had to talk about it until he could trust me enough to go on. Gradually Zachary began to believe that I might be interested enough in him to help him. He began to realize that he was anticipating a lack of interest coming from me and that was causing him to see me as disinterested at times when I might not be. In fact, my willingness to weather all of his attacks began to give Zachary the impression that I might find something about him worth the price he was asking me to pay. It was through the process of constantly repairing our relationship that Zachary began to think about how he might be able to approach his relationships outside of therapy differently. Eventually, he even began to rethink his mother's motives for acting the way she did.

"She always was an introvert," he mused in one session. "She may have been too shy to participate in things at school or too afraid to share her emotions verbally. I guess I don't really know if my mother disliked me or not—she just never let me know what she was thinking."

Zachary has decided to approach his mother about a different kind of relationship, one that includes more honest talking about feelings and fewer meaningless conversations just to fill the time. He has decided that he doesn't always know what his mother is thinking based upon her behavior, and the truth is, he feels bad about the broken relationship between the two of them. Zachary has learned in his therapy that restoring broken relationships can heal something inside of him personally. If repairing his relationship with his therapist could be helpful, a man who was a stranger to him until a few years ago, think how much more helpful it could be in repairing his relationship with his mother, the most influential person in his life.

The mission of Jesus was to restore broken relationships between people and God. He was sent by God, because "God so loved the world," to personally reconcile everyone to God. The purpose of his religion was to provide a vehicle to make this possible. To him, establishing a personal relationship with God was the key to spiritual wholeness.

Many psychologists view the key to psychological health in much the same way. Their mission is to correct the damage done by broken relationships, and therapy is their vehicle to make this possible. To them, establishing an emotional relationship is the key to psychological wholeness. You might say that the psychologist's mission of restoring broken relationships on a horizontal level, human to human, is parallel to Jesus' spiritual mission of restoring broken vertical relationships, between humans with God. In this way the missions of both Jesus and psychology have something very much in common.

> **SPIRITUAL PRINCIPLE:** Mending broken relationships is
> partnering with God.

FORGIVENESS AND HEALING

"Which is easier: to say, 'Your sins are forgiven,' or to say,
'Get up and walk'?"
Luke 5:23

Abused and abandoned by her parents as a child, Emma grew up in the foster-care system. Her childhood was unusually difficult because of the treatment she received from her parents as well as in several of her placements. Emma had always blamed her parents for the suffering she had to endure, but lately she has decided to put all that behind her.

"I'm over it," she explained to me. "They were probably just kids who couldn't handle the responsibility, or they were just too broke, or something. It doesn't matter. I just focus on the present and leave the past in the past. I'm not interested in a lot of 'navel-gazing' therapy. I just need a few quick sessions to get me back on the track."

But Emma's past wasn't staying in the past. She was angry much of the time, mistrusted people, never slept well, and also made consistently bad choices in her relationships. Emma had *excused* her parents, but she hadn't *forgiven* them. She wanted to move on, so she didn't want to look back. Digging up all those painful memories of her childhood was just too much work for too little reward in her mind.

As it turned out, Emma's therapy wasn't as "quick" as she had hoped. It took years of therapy and support groups before Emma could realize the importance of dealing with her unfinished business with her parents, much less even think about forgiving them. Quite frankly, she didn't believe they deserved it. Emma didn't want to forgive her parents because she thought that would make what they did okay. It doesn't. It is perfectly fine to forgive people but choose to never let them back into your life if you don't believe having them there would be a good thing. Emma needed to believe that what they did was wrong, but she didn't have to keep hating them for it. Her hatred was only hurting herself. Emma needed to forgive her parents for her own sake, not theirs.

Emma has shared in her therapy and support groups how it felt growing up, enough to believe that she isn't alone with her feelings anymore. Because she believes others understand how she felt, Emma has been given the courage to look at her resentment of her parents in new ways. Now, instead of excusing them and then secretly hating them for what they did, Emma has done the hard task of forgiving them even though they don't deserve it. In doing so she has released them, and herself, from a lifetime of blame and hatred. It was a lot of work, but it couldn't have happened any other way for Emma. Emma knows she has forgiven her parents because she wishes them well, wherever they are. Emma has done the hard work of forgiveness and brought about a deeper level of spiritual and psychological wholeness in her life because of it.

Sometimes my patients come for psychotherapy wanting an instant solution to their problems. They would like me to say something miraculous that will allow them to psychologically "get up and walk" instantaneously. The truth is, when we have been wounded at our deepest level, we are in need of a process that requires our active participation. We need to do the work of identifying the brokenness in our hearts and relationships and following through with forgiveness. This is usually not easy, and rarely instantaneous. In the long run, the type of healing that comes through the process of forgiveness and making peace with the past is the most profound pathway to spiritual and psychological wholeness.

People were interested in the instant solutions at the time of Jesus as well. They wanted miracles rather than hard work. But Jesus wasn't interested in simply helping people feel better—he wanted them to get better. To him that meant dealing with the wounds in our hearts and relationships that required the hard work of forgiveness and reconciliation. He knew that sometimes it was actually easier to tell someone physically debilitated to "get up and walk" than it was to say, "Your sins are forgiven." Physically healing the body was easy compared to the repentance and forgiveness needed in human hearts.

SPIRITUAL PRINCIPLE: Excusing people is easier than forgiving them—but not better.

CHAPTER 10

KNOWING YOUR
PERSONAL POWER

When a Samaritan woman came to draw water, Jesus said to her, "Will you give me a drink?"

The Samaritan woman said to him, "You are a Jew and I am a Samaritan woman. How can you ask me for a drink?" . . .

Jesus answered, "Everyone who drinks this water will be thirsty again, but whoever drinks the water I give him will never thirst." . . .

The woman said to him, "Sir, give me this water so that I won't get thirsty." . . .

He told her, "Go, call your husband and come back."

"I have no husband," she replied.

Jesus said to her, "You are right when you say you have no husband. The fact is, you have had five husbands, and the man you now have is not your husband."

"Sir," the woman said, "I can see that you are a prophet. . . . I know that Messiah is coming. When he comes, he will explain everything to us."

Then Jesus declared, "I who speak to you am he."

Just then his disciples returned and were surprised to find him talking with a woman. But no one asked, . . . "Why are you talking with her?"

Then, leaving her water jar, the woman went back to the town and said to the people, "Come, see a man who told me everything I ever did. Could this be the Christ?"

John 4:7–30

There is something intoxicating about achieving power *over* others, but its effect is only temporary. Jesus had the eternally satisfying experience in life of achieving power *with* others. To him, personal power was power with other people. This was frustrating for the followers of Jesus, because many of them expected him to establish himself as a political ruler and appoint them to positions of influence in his new reign. Jesus knew that the truly powerful person is more interested in people than politics. For him, the true test of personal power is not in controlling others, but empowering them.

Even though he was one of the greatest religious leaders in history, Jesus spent very little time in religious settings. The vast majority of his time was spent where people lived. He was interested in people and was a very influential person in the lives of the people he met.

Jesus knew that empathy was the secret to true personal power. Empathy is not having feelings of sympathy for others, but sustaining an interest in them. This then allows for a true understanding. When empathy is utilized well, the result can be transforming.[1]

THE DEFINITION OF PERSONAL POWER

"Give to Caesar what is Caesar's, and to God what is God's."
Matthew 22:21

Justin is a powerful man. He is a high-ranking government official, has several graduate degrees, and is nationally known because of his career in politics. Justin put himself through college and worked his way up to the position he now holds. He is proud of his accomplishments because he doesn't expect others to give him breaks as much as he expects to create them for himself.

Because he was afraid it might hurt his career, Justin made sure no one knew he was coming for therapy. In the world of political sharks in which he lived, receiving therapy might be perceived as a weakness for which he could get eaten alive.

My first task was to educate Justin on how to make use of personal therapy. It isn't a place where we fix people. This was a new concept for Justin. He was used to identifying obstacles and overcoming them. But Justin didn't need me to give him advice to fix his problems. He needed me to help him understand himself better so that he could come up with better advice for himself.

Although Justin was a powerful man in many ways, he thought of power in hierarchical terms. To him, power was used to get to the top. Justin thought of power as a scarce commodity—the more he had, the less the other person would have. He was constantly trying to balance the power in his relationships, figuring that if he gave up too much of it he was going to end up in the weaker position. This resulted in continual power struggles in Justin's personal relationships.

What Justin and I are coming to in our therapy together is a different experience of power. Although he first felt threatened by the power differential in our relationship, he feels that less now. He is starting to realize that I can be powerful in his life in a way that empowers him. It isn't my techniques or suggestions on how to do things that empower Justin as much as it is the insights we come to together as a result of our relationship. Justin initially felt I had power *over* him because I am a doctor and he pays me. But he is starting to experience my power *with* him because our relationship helps him to better understand himself. My knowing him helps him know himself better. Justin is beginning to learn that my having power in his life is a good thing for him. He is starting to understand personal power in the way that Jesus intended it.

There are many different types of power—physical, political, financial, intellectual, spiritual, personal—the list is long. Although some people pursue power in all of its forms, Jesus was only interested in the type of power that lasts. He was interested in genuine personal power.

Some think of personal power as something emanating from within the individual, like a force enabling someone to achieve his or her personal individual best. Jesus didn't think of it in that way. To Jesus, personal power was a connection with other people that resulted in something much more than an individual's best. Personal power is a spiritual union between people that makes each person more than he or she could be individually. Personal power is something that grows as you give it away because it doesn't come from within individuals—it is something that is created between them.

Jesus knew that Caesar was interested in a type of power that would die out when he did, which is why he said, "Give to Caesar what is Caesar's." Jesus was interested in power that goes beyond the grave. To him personal power was power *with* other persons, not over them or even within them. He thought it was a mistake to try to get power for oneself. The type of power he wanted for us could only be felt by giving it away.

SPIRITUAL PRINCIPLE: Personal power is power *with* other people, not *over* them.

THE POWER OF BEING KNOWN PERSONALLY

"I know you."
John 5:42

Olivia came to therapy to work on her self-esteem. She knew she wasn't as confident as she needed to be, and she wanted to overcome her shyness. She had read a few books on self-esteem and had tried to practice their suggestions with moderate success. Even though she could instruct herself to change her thinking about things, she was still left with feelings of self-doubt.

Olivia wanted to make the most out of her time with me, so she asked me for a homework assignment at the end of our first session.

"I'd like to work on my self-esteem a little bit every day," she said, "so anything you could give me to do would help me learn how to deal with this problem faster."

"It seems you already know quite a bit about self-esteem," I replied. "Perhaps what you need to learn more about at this point is yourself, and I think we both need to be present to make that happen."

I could see that what Olivia needed was not more information, but personal knowledge. The process of more deeply understanding herself would come through the experience of being known. Over the course of the next several months this is exactly what happened for her.

Through our therapy together, I discovered that Olivia thought she knew quite a bit about herself. The problem was that she felt bad about who she was. Because of this, she rarely opened up to people and kept the negative feelings a secret for fear that others would feel the same way about her. Unfortunately, secrets kept hidden rarely change. Reading more about how she *should* be only made her feel worse about who she *was*. What she needed was to bring her secrets out into the open with another person so that she could feel personally known. This was the starting point for the transformation of her self-esteem. Pretending to be someone she wanted to be was building the foundation of her self-image on shifting sand. She needed to feel that who she was now was a good enough start and that she could add upon the truth of who she was and still be okay.

Olivia's therapy hasn't been what she thought it was going to be. However, I think it has been more powerful than what she had imagined. She has shifted her focus of interest in our time together from acquiring information from me to being known by me. I certainly don't experience Olivia as shy anymore, and others are seeing a difference as well. I believe Olivia is becoming more personally powerful because she is feeling understood, and it doesn't feel as bad as she feared it would. In fact, as scary as it sometimes is, I think Olivia would say it actually feels good.

Humans cannot survive in isolation, and as a result we strive to connect with others. Just as we know that there is physical safety in numbers, the experience of being known gives us the psychological sense that all is well. We must have the sense of being known by others in order to develop properly. We need to feel that we are known not only for what we do, but for who we are in order to be psychologically whole. This kind of knowledge is not something contained within an individual's mind; it is something that is shared between people. Personal knowledge takes two people to create, and it leaves each of them changed once it has been created. The experience of knowing and being known is the starting point for personal power.

Jesus believed that we were created for the purpose of knowing God and being known by him. Jesus' followers referred to him as the "Word" of God, or the ultimate communication from God to humankind. A central aspect of his teaching was to communicate the life-transforming power of knowing God, which was not an intellectual knowledge, but a relational experience.

SPIRITUAL PRINCIPLE: Personal knowledge is created between people; not within them.

THE POWER OF EMPATHY

"Come, see a man who told me everything I ever did."
John 4:29

John was forced to come to therapy because of his difficulty getting along with people. He was about to lose his job, and his wife was threatening to divorce him. He didn't like psychologists and thought therapy was a waste of money. But if he didn't show some sign of attempting to do something about his problem, he was afraid his wife really would leave him, and that would make things even worse.

I found John to be the type of person who is difficult for me to like. He felt entitled to be rude to people, was often threatening, and believed in winning by intimidation. John often confronted me in our sessions about various things as if he were looking for an argument. He was pugnacious, and proud of it.

In spite of the fact that I couldn't identify with John and it was difficult for me to feel compassion for the difficulties he created for himself, I did come to understand him over time. He had suffered a number of painful humiliations in his life and was angry because of it. Although he wasn't extremely open with me about the nature of his past traumas, I came to understand enough to help John see that his frequent rages at current events in his life had something to do with past events over which he still felt a need for vengeance. He had been hurt, and somebody needed to pay.

I would like to be able to say that I became a Christlike figure to John in our therapy together and that he was healed of his anger because of it, but in many respects I fell short of what Jesus would have done. I did, however, do one thing that was helpful for John. I understood him enough to help him come to know himself a little better, and as a result he did change. He left therapy with a better grasp of why he gets as angry as he does and with some strategies for coping with his feelings differently. I wouldn't call John cured, but I would say that he has greatly improved. Even though it was difficult for me, the empathic understanding of John's pain made a difference in his life. John found the impact of empathy impossible to escape.

The woman at the well was so profoundly moved by Jesus' empathic understanding of her that she felt as if he knew "everything she ever did." This was how Jesus demonstrated his personal power. He showed his miraculous, spiritual, and intellectual power at other times, but he had a special love for communicating personal power through his empathy for others.

Jesus had the ability to impress large crowds with amazing displays of divine authority, but he was most interested in making contact with each individual personally. He did not see his greatest miracles on earth as having to do with physical displays of supernatural power;[2] he saw them as those moments when his empathic connection with human hearts left lives changed forever. Empathy is understanding, and no one in history has displayed a greater capacity for it than Jesus.

SPIRITUAL PRINCIPLE: The greatest expression of empathy is to be understanding of someone you dislike.

THE POWER OF SYMPATHY

"For God so loved the world . . ."
John 3:16

I supervise a number of student therapists at the counseling center where I work. I love working with beginning therapists because they bring such enthusiasm to the practice of psychotherapy. Of course, therapists just getting started in their practice don't have much experience, but I have found that what they lack in experience they make up for in compassion for their patients.

One of my supervisees, Mary, was given as one of her first patients a woman, Connie, who had come from a terrible upbringing. Connie had never been in therapy before and had never spoken to another human being about the abusive molestation she had suffered as a child. As their therapy progressed, Connie began to feel safe enough to share with Mary the experiences she had kept secret her entire life. Her accounts of humiliating abuse and degradation were painful for even Mary to hear, but they both somehow knew that the retelling of Connie's story was an essential part of her healing.

During one session, although she was afraid it was unprofessional, Mary couldn't help herself—she began to cry. By the end of the session both Connie and Mary were looking at each other with tear-filled eyes. They then discussed how painful it was for Connie to have survived her childhood—and to have done it alone. Mary felt genuine compassion for Connie, and they both knew it.

Over the course of our supervision together, Mary and I discovered that her spontaneous tears with Connie actually turned out to be quite therapeutic. Connie had been afraid to share her story because she felt too ashamed of it. She was fearful that anyone hearing about her molestation would be angry with her, like her mother was when Connie accused her father of such a despicable thing. Mary's tears sent her quite a different message. Connie took Mary's willingness to cry with her as a sign that her abuse wasn't her fault and that she could be loved even at the moments when she felt the least lovable. Connie was afraid that her negative feelings made her bad, but Mary's sympathy for her made her feel valuable enough to be cared for even if she didn't value herself.

Both Mary and Connie discovered something that Jesus taught centuries ago. Compassion gives us personal power. In Mary's case it gave her the personal power to facilitate healing in Connie's life that no one had ever done before.

Sympathy is not empathy. Sympathy is the feeling of compassion for another that can take the form of warmth, mercy, or even pity. We can feel sympathy for people even if we don't understand them. Jesus felt a loving-kindness for others out of the generosity of his heart. Sympathy was an aspect of his personal power.

Jesus did not come into the world because he found humankind disgusting. He came because "God so loved the world." He never approached people with the attitude that they needed to change in order to be lovable. No one needed to do anything to earn his love, because he loved them for who they were, including any imperfections they may have had. Jesus was personally powerful because he was sympathetic toward people.

SPIRITUAL PRINCIPLE: What you lack in knowledge, you can make up for in compassion.

THE POWER TO IDENTIFY WITH OTHERS

"Because I live, you also will live."
John 14:19

Several years ago a friend of mine called me and told me that he was turning forty. I said I was sorry. He then went on to tell me that he was going to take a trip to Milwaukee, and he wanted to know if I would like to go along.

"Milwaukee?" I asked. "Why?"

"Because," he explained, "Milwaukee is known for two things: beer and Harley-Davidsons."

"I'm in," I said.

By the time my friend and I actually got to Milwaukee to purchase our brand-new Harley-Davidson motorcycles we were going to ride back to California, we had twenty-eight other friends with us. It was the largest private sale of Harley-Davidsons the dealer in Milwaukee had ever seen.

We were mostly a group of professional men (a couple of psychologists, a dentist, a couple of ministers, an accountant, and so on), but we enjoyed the experience of doing something quite out of our professional arenas for a couple of weeks. On the way back, we started every day with a prayer asking God to allow us to survive the road trip that day. None of us had ever ridden Harleys before. Even the nonreligious guys in the group were praying by the end of the trip. There's something about the feeling of facing death that gives one an appreciation for life.

In one small town we decided to see a movie that had just been released that week. We lined our Harleys up outside the movie theater and filed in. I overheard one kid in front of us whisper to his friend, "Hey, there's bikers in here!" before they got up and moved. It actually felt great to be identified with such a powerful group of guys. But at the Harley dealership the next day I found myself standing next to a rather large, tattooed, rough-hewn member of a certain motorcycle club (whose name shall go unmentioned) as my companions were dismounting their shiny new bikes. I was a bit dismayed to overhear him ask his buddy, "Are these a bunch of businessmen on a trip or something?" Perhaps we didn't appear as dangerously powerful to everyone we encountered.

I learned something about identification on that trip. Many of the men in the group I had never met before, and I didn't learn much about them over the course of our time together. The thing about riding Harleys is that you can't talk. For most men, that makes it the perfect thing to do together. But by the end of the two weeks I felt a powerful bond with those men. We had done something very unusual together that had created intense feelings in each of us that could only be known through experience. We could identify with each other because we knew what we had all gone through. At times we literally trusted each other with our lives. We had this type of personal power with each other because of the identity we had shared.

Identification is not the same thing as empathy or sympathy. Identification is having the same personal experience as someone else. You may not have ever discussed what the other person was thinking or feeling, but there is a powerful kinship between people who have had the same experience. We trust others who can identify with our pain even if we don't know them.

Jesus wanted to personally know what people experienced in life. The God he talked about did not remain in heaven and send down edicts from a distant world above. He sent his son to personally live out a human existence so he could know firsthand what it was like. Although Jesus was making a point about spiritual life when he said, "Because I live, you also will live," he was also making a profound psychological observation about personal power at the same time. Jesus was personally powerful with others because he went through the same struggles as those he cared about. Jesus could identify with the pain of others because he had been there.[3] Identification was an aspect of the personal power of Jesus.

SPIRITUAL PRINCIPLE: Experience can communicate a bond that can't be expressed in words.

PEOPLE OR POLITICS?

"The greatest among you will be your servant."
Matthew 23:11

Halle was a successful businesswoman who had demonstrated that a woman could be effective in a male-dominated industry, but her successful career had come with a price. Knowing she would not be taken seriously in the cutthroat executive meetings she led if she became "too emotional," Halle had mastered the skill of repressing her feelings. She was very effective at accomplishing her goals for the corporation, but the goals she had for herself had become eclipsed.

In our therapy together, Halle and I uncovered a few paradoxes in her life. One was that she was being forced to make decisions that were in her best interests politically, but not in her best interests emotionally. Not saying how she felt about the unfair and sometimes cruel business practices of her associates preserved her position in the organization, but at the same time it resulted in the deterioration of her psychological health. On the other hand, speaking up about her feelings might be the right thing to do emotionally, but it could cost her her job.

As we examined the multiple dimensions in the choices Halle was making in her life, she came to a difficult conclusion. Although she saw a bright future for herself if she continued to make political correctness the most important variable in her career decisions, she concluded that she could not support remaining on the same career path based upon most of the other variables she considered. All the people who were important in her life were suffering because of her choices, including herself. It was the people she respected least who were benefiting the most. Halle decided this was not the way she wanted to live. She decided she could not have a meaningful life as long as she chose politics over people.

Today, Halle is a successful executive for a nonprofit organization, and she loves her job. She has scaled down her lifestyle economically to match the decrease in her salary when she left the private sector, but she has upgraded her lifestyle in terms of the amount and quality of time she spends with the people she loves. Halle isn't as anxious or depressed as she once was; in fact, she is actually happy most days. Happiness isn't a feeling she used to consider in her decision-making process a few years ago, but it's one she puts at the top of her decision tree today.

Sometimes the political, moral, spiritual, and psychological ramifications of our decisions may be at odds with each other, and we may have to choose between them. Someone else may not have had to make the decision to change jobs that Halle did. There is no one answer to these personal dilemmas, but in Halle's case political correctness wasn't worth the price she was having to pay.

Ambition motivates people to seek political power. People are ambitious for a number of reasons, some of which are quite healthy and good. Personal power, however, is motivated by love. Jesus was willing to sacrifice the politically correct thing to preserve his personal power.

Even those closest to Jesus did not understand his personal power. His disciples argued among themselves over who would be the greatest in his impending political reign.[4] Surely, they thought, someone as powerful as Jesus would rise to whatever political position of fame and fortune he pleased. But Jesus chose people over politics when he said, "The greatest among you will be your servant." To him, personal power would always be lived out that way.

SPIRITUAL PRINCIPLE: Political correctness has a personal price.

THE POWER OF TRUE SELF-ESTEEM

"For I know where I came from and where I am going."
John 8:14

In the summer of 1941, during World War II, a young sergeant named James Allen Ward was awarded the Victoria Cross for his act of heroism. In the middle of one battle, the starboard engine of his Wellington bomber burst into flames as a result of enemy fire. With the lives of the men on board in his hands, Ward climbed out onto the wing of the airplane at 13,000 feet, secured only by a rope around his waist. Struggling against the wind and enemy attacks, he put out the fire and crawled back on his hands and knees into the fuselage of the airplane.

When Winston Churchill learned of this, he summoned the shy New Zealander to his home at 10 Downing Street. Churchill loved to reward such acts of courage and personally thank the men and women responsible. When Churchill tried to strike up a conversation, he found Ward so awestruck by being in the prime minister's presence that he couldn't answer any of his questions.

Churchill then said, "You must feel very humble and awkward in my presence."

Looking down at his feet, Ward quietly replied, "Yes, sir. I do."

Without hesitating Churchill said, "Then you can imagine how awkward and humble I feel in yours."

Winston Churchill displayed true self-esteem. This was obvious by the way he treated Ward. True self-esteem inspires the same in others. False self-esteem leaves others feeling less adequate. True self-esteem empowers, while false self-esteem attempts to control.

It is impossible to have too much true self-esteem. Those who appear to "love themselves too much," or be overly self-confident, are actually suffering from false self-esteem. False self-esteem is arrogance that draws attention to oneself. True self-esteem is confident self-assurance that frees one to give attention to others.

Because Jesus was confidant about who he was, he could be open to others; he did not have to impress them. In fact, he doubted the sincerity of those who followed him simply because he was able to do impressive things. He wasn't interested in controlling people with his power. He was confident enough to know that genuine personal power grows out of being open enough to let others get to know who you are. Jesus didn't listen to others because he was shy, he didn't serve them because he felt bad about himself, and he didn't draw them out because he was afraid he had nothing to say. Jesus made other people feel good because he felt good about himself. This is the power of true self-esteem.

It is very difficult to be personally powerful. Most people will seek out some other form of power instead. Jesus had personal power, which was obvious from his true self-esteem. He said, "For I know where I came from and where I am going." Because he knew who he was, he was confident enough in his identity to turn the focus of his attention on others.

SPIRITUAL PRINCIPLE: True self-esteem esteems others.

THE DIFFERENCE BETWEEN CONFIDENCE AND ARROGANCE

"They that take the sword shall perish with the sword."
Matthew 26:52 (King James Version)

Brian had read a lot of books on self-confidence. He believed in maximizing his potential, winning by intimidation, and programming himself for success. To him, self-confidence was the inner force allowing him to achieve his personal best without feeling bad about himself in the process.

Brian's concept of self-confidence was motivating him to work hard in his career without the many distractions of self-doubt. His personal life however, was deteriorating in the process. His friends were being replaced by business associates and networking opportunities. People were starting to fear him more than like him, and the women in his life were not working out at a faster and faster rate. Even though Brian said he liked himself more than he ever had before, everyone else seemed to like him less.

Gradually over the course of his personal therapy, Brian came to realize that his notions about self-confidence were an attempt to cover up a lack of it. He didn't want more things because he felt good about himself; he wanted them because without them he felt bad. He was trying to cover over bad feelings rather than pursue good ones. Brian is starting to redefine self-confidence in his life. It's defined more by personal contentment than personal success. His focus is less on trying to get somewhere and more on trying to be right where he is in a more authentic way.

Ironically, Brian is realizing that his pursuit of his personal best wasn't improving his self-confidence; it was making him arrogant. Focusing on being better than others never made him feel better about who he was at the time. Feeling good about himself was something he had to take by force from the world, not something that came naturally or with ease.

Brian is beginning to understand what Jesus meant when he said, "They that take the sword shall perish with the sword." Constantly viewing the world as a psychological battleground where only the strong survive was forcing him to base his view of himself on what he did rather than who he was. The problem with a performance-based concept of self-confidence is that you feel only as good as your last performance. Victories in this war were building up his arrogance rather than his self-confidence, and this was driving people away. Brian is starting to base his self-confidence on being a more authentic person, and this is drawing people nearer. Brian is still an extremely successful businessman on his way to the top of his profession, but he doesn't want to be all alone when he gets there.

People knew immediately that Jesus had personal power. There was no mistaking that this was a man with self-confidence. His powerful presence allowed him to be confident enough to captivate crowds of thousands or focus his attention on the smallest child with complete comfort. He had the unique ability to communicate a powerful confidence without being mistaken for a man with an arrogant need for control.

There is a simple test to know if you are in the presence of someone who is arrogant or someone who is self-confident. When you are in the presence of someone who has true self-esteem and is self-confident, you feel empowered. When you are in the presence of someone who has false self-esteem and is trying to compensate for that with arrogance, you feel overpowered. Jesus did not need others to feel worse about themselves so that he could feel better about himself. He left people feeling grateful they had met him.

SPIRITUAL PRINCIPLE: Confidence empowers, while arrogance overpowers.

THE PRICE OF PERSONAL POWER

"The greatest love is shown when a person lays down his life
for his friends."
John 15:13 *(Living Bible)*

The Russian author Fyodor Dostoyevsky has written some psychologically powerful novels. In one of my favorites, he writes about a prince named Myshkin who has a naive but refreshing approach to life. Because Myshkin is completely vulnerable to everyone, he finds himself being the brunt of many jokes and subject to much abuse because of it. As the story progresses, we find that Prince Myshkin's childlike openness to others becomes a kind of goodness in the midst of a world full of deceit and selfishness. He becomes a Christlike figure whom we find ourselves admiring for his honesty. Ironically, Dostoyevsky titles the book *The Idiot.*

Dostoyevsky was making a point. To commit ourselves to a lifestyle of vulnerability may result in personal power, but it comes with a price. Prince Myshkin was as powerful as he was in the lives of those he met because he was vulnerable to them. Those who would take advantage of him did, and those who chose to learn from him benefited from doing so. Prince Myshkin could not control how others were going to respond to him; nor did he try. He merely chose to be vulnerable in a world of hardness, which made him personally powerful in the lives of those he met. We are all fools for something. Prince Myshkin was willing to be viewed as an idiot in order to have personal power.

Understanding others does not come easily, and sometimes we must contain our own thoughts and feelings in order to do it. Vulnerability is the prerequisite to the empathic understanding of others, which is the key to personal power. However, we must be willing to open ourselves up in order to get others to open up to us. This is the paradox of personal power. It is only when we are vulnerable that we can achieve personal power with others, and it is exactly when we are vulnerable that we can be most injured by them. The vulnerability required makes understanding others dangerous work. This kind of vulnerability is the price of personal power.

Jesus referred to the price of personal power when he said, "The greatest love is shown when a person lays down his life for his friends." He knew that to achieve personal power people would have to pay a price. Jesus was personally powerful with others because he was willing to pay the price of being vulnerable. He not only preached about this truth—he lived it.

SPIRITUAL PRINCIPLE: Vulnerability is both the path and the price for power with others.

CHAPTER 11

KNOWING YOUR CENTERED SELF

As Jesus and the disciples continued on their way to Jerusalem
they came to a village where a woman named Martha wel-
comed them into her home. Her sister Mary sat on the floor, lis-
tening to Jesus as he talked.

But Martha was the jittery type and was worrying over the
big dinner she was preparing. She came to Jesus and said, "Sir,
doesn't it seem unfair to you that my sister just sits here while I
do all the work? Tell her to come and help me."

But the Lord said to her, "Martha, dear friend, you are so
upset over all these details! There is really only one thing worth
being concerned about. Mary has discovered it—and I won't
take it away from her!"

Luke 10:38–42 (Living Bible)

Although Martha thought Mary was being self-centered in failing to
help her, she was actually spiritually centering herself by focusing upon
her relationship with Jesus. The paradox in the teachings of Jesus was
that we could only find our spiritual center within through our relationship with God who was outside of us. His term for that was righteousness. Spiritual righteousness involves relying upon someone greater
than ourselves. Self-righteousness involves relying only upon ourselves.
As it turned out, Martha was the one being self-centered when she
thought she was being righteous.

Jesus defined righteousness as having a right relationship with God.
Many people, like Martha, are not quite sure what this means, so they
look for ways to reassure themselves that they are in good standing
with God and end up becoming self-righteous in the process. Jesus
knew that the centered self doesn't come through efforts toward making ourselves righteous; it comes through having relationships that are

right. Our good deeds flow out of our righteousness, not the other way around.

The term "righteousness" can apply to our relationships with other people as well as to our relationship with God. To have right relationships with others we must see our need for them as a sign of strength, not weakness.[1] It is only through our relationships with God and others that we can achieve our greatest potential and find a centered self. When we try to do things solely on our own, we end up like Martha, feeling self-righteous and dissatisfied with our self-centered lives.

RIGHTEOUSNESS

"There is really only one thing worth being concerned about."
Luke 10:42 (Living Bible)

"Do you pray with your patients?" Phillip asked.

"That depends upon the patient," I replied. "Do you pray with your doctors?"

"Not anymore," Phillip said brusquely. Even though I had only known Phillip for a few minutes, he was telling me a lot about himself already.

Phillip had been in therapy before with a Christian psychologist. Since he had been told that I was also a Christian, he was trying to find out if his treatment with me would be something like what he had experienced before.

"I'm sure he was a really good therapist and all, but I just didn't do well with Dr. Richmond," Phillip said. "He knew exactly what was wrong with me and what I should do to change. But I guess I just didn't want to change bad enough. I didn't want to waste his time or my money, so I quit."

Phillip is a Christian who does well in most areas of his life, but he has a private struggle with which he would like help. Although he has never acted on them, he has occasional suicidal thoughts, which are quite disturbing to him.

"I know the Bible says it's a sin to kill someone, even yourself," he cried, "but I get so depressed sometimes that the idea of ending my own life just pops into my head. I really don't want to have these feelings, but simply telling myself that they are wrong doesn't make them go away."

Phillip was tormented by feelings he didn't understand. He didn't want to die, but he couldn't help thinking about death sometimes in ways that made him very uncomfortable. He was desperately trying to control his feelings of depression and thoughts of suicide, which only made him feel more depressed.

Ending his own life became the one thing he could think of to ultimately control his emotional struggle. Ironically, he thought killing himself might be the only way to rid himself of his sinful suicidal thoughts. He believed that the Bible and his previous therapist were telling him he should simply renounce these feelings and choose to feel differently about himself. Phillip believed that righteousness was choosing the right thing to do, and he felt ashamed of himself because he simply wasn't able to do it in this area of his life.

I was able to help Phillip, in part because I didn't define righteousness in the same way he did. Telling ourselves the right thing to do and then living up to that by the strength of our own willpower is not my idea of righteousness. As a psychologist, I prefer the idea of righteousness as making our relationships with God and others as right as we can.

Because of where Phillip was in his relationship to his faith and because of his past experiences in therapy, I took the emphasis off what he should be *doing* in our work together and put it on who he *was* as a man. Instead of focusing upon how he was failing to live up to standards of righteousness or psychological health, we focused upon his feelings and what had happened in his life that might be contributing to them. We discovered some interesting things.

First, we discovered that he was not sinful or sick for having the feelings he did. In fact, we found that his feelings of depression came out of previous experiences that could explain why he felt the way he did. As Phillip understood where his feelings of depression came from, he was less tormented by them and stopped trying to control them so much. He began to see his feelings of depression as a part of his life that would naturally come and go, which made him feel less out of control and less in need of some desperate action to stop these "sinful" feelings. As time went on, we discovered that Phillip wasn't really as interested in forcing himself to do and think the right things as he was in feeling that he was a man with integrity, one who struggles to honestly deal with himself. And eventually we discovered that as Phillip felt less out of control of himself, he had fewer suicidal thoughts as well.

It turned out in Phillip's life that his suicidal feelings were not the problem. They were only the symptom. Focusing upon the symptom of his behavior that was disturbing didn't seem to help him. Focusing upon his feelings about himself, his therapist, and his God did. Trying to force himself to live up to some technical standard of righteousness wasn't helping Phillip. Trying to work out a relationship that felt right with me, and God, did.

Jesus understood what we have discovered in psychological theory: the connection is central to the cure. Being technically right according to our psychological theory at the expense of the relationship with the patient is like the brain surgeon who takes delight in the success of the operation even though his patient died. Not that our theories are not important; in fact, it is because they are so important that we need to constantly consider the impact they are making on our patients and be prepared to sacrifice our theories before we sacrifice our patients.

From Jesus' perspective, righteousness is maintaining right relationships, and sin is anything we do that separates us from God and others. This has always been confusing for religious people who define righteousness as having to do with right behavior rather than right relationships.

Jesus always made people a priority. He didn't believe that legalistic accuracy could improve the condition of the human heart. He defined righteousness as an attitude of the heart rather than faultless behavior. This is why Martha was mistaken in thinking her "doing" for Jesus was somehow better than Mary's interest in simply "being" with him. When it comes to righteousness, "There is really only one thing worth being concerned about."

SPIRITUAL PRINCIPLE: Righteousness is right relationships.

ONLY SINNERS CAN BE RIGHTEOUS

*"If any one of you is without sin, let him be the first to throw
a stone at her."*
John 8:7

Dalton and Miranda seemed like a great couple. They were both attractive, fun-loving people. They had a great house and cute kids, and everyone loved to go to their parties. As far as appearances went, everything looked pretty good for them.

But appearances can be deceiving. Miranda knew Dalton was a great guy, but she wasn't as happy with him as everyone else seemed to be. Sure, he was fun, but he was better at telling his stories than listening to hers. She loved that he was so good-looking, but he was in too much of a hurry when it came to sex. Miranda knew she had married the "life of the party," but she wanted something more. She wanted to go to those quiet places in her heart with her husband and feel deeply understood. Miranda wanted more intimacy, and she just didn't think Dalton had it to give.

Miranda didn't realize what was happening at first, but she found herself having intense, personal conversations with one of their neighbors on an increasingly regular basis. Sheldon was a friend of both Dalton and Miranda, and one Miranda found it especially easy to talk to. "We just clicked," she explained later. "It was as if I had known Sheldon my entire life. Talking to him was effortless. Nothing seemed more natural." At some point Miranda realized that she was having an emotional affair. She wasn't being intimate with Sheldon physically, but she was certainly giving him the intimate parts of her emotional self.

Dalton and Miranda made the wise choice to come for marriage counseling to deal with their situation. She had confessed the nature of her relationship with Sheldon and agreed to break it off with him in order to find out if her marriage could be saved.

Dalton was deeply hurt and angry because he hadn't really done anything wrong. When it comes to affairs, if you aren't left because of what you did, then you must be left for who you are—a very painful thing to endure.

Dalton, however, rose to the occasion. Perhaps it was partly his competitive side coming out (not wanting to lose to Sheldon) and partly his genuine love for the woman he married, but Dalton fought back. Dalton fought for his wife and his family, but not in a defensive, destructive way. It took great effort to risk telling her how humiliated he was, but he didn't stop until he was sure she understood the depth of his pain and anger. He fought to listen to how lonely she felt in their marriage and struggled to understand his role in that. Dalton was often tempted to throw stones at Miranda, but he restrained himself from being hurtful simply because he had been hurt. He knew he wasn't perfect, and he wasn't going to make things better by trying to pretend he was.

Somewhere in the process of our marital counseling, Dalton learned something about himself. He could be both angry and loving at the same time. Dalton was learning to be truly passionate. He learned that the opposite of love was not anger, but apathy, and he had been guilty of that in his relationship with Miranda.

Miranda learned some things about herself too. She learned that secretly taking things that didn't belong to her (Sheldon was married too) or giving away things that were not hers to give was a selfish solution to her problems. She found that she had not been as open a person as she thought she was and that she had judged Dalton unfairly as being psychologically inferior. But most important, Miranda learned that she could be loved at a time in her life when she deserved it least. Once she came to understand how deeply Dalton had been hurt by her affair, she was amazed at how much he still loved her anyway.

Miranda and Dalton are a success story in marriage counseling. They came as imperfect people who had both contributed to the hurt in their marriage. In acknowledging this, they were admitting that they were both "sinners" in Jesus' terminology. Acknowledging where they had been wrong was the starting place for making things right. Their marriage is a "work-in-progress" today. Their communication is better, the feelings of love are more intense, and they would both say their marriage is better than it has ever been. Their marriage isn't perfect, but it is certainly righteous in the way that Jesus understood relationships should be.

On one occasion a woman who was caught in the act of adultery was brought to Jesus so that certain religious leaders could test his respect for their doctrines. For Jesus to be viewed as a righteous man, he had to follow Jewish law, which specifically demanded that she be stoned to death. But Jesus had a different view of righteousness. He asked each person in the crowd to look into their own hearts by saying, "If any one of you is without sin, let him be the first to throw a stone at her." There was no stoning that day.

By doing this, Jesus was clarifying his definition of righteousness. Righteous people followed religious laws because they *already* were in relationship with God, not in order to *make* themselves righteous. Human beings often get things turned around. Out of our own insecurity we take guidelines intended to help us keep our relationships intact and turn them into rules that we can use to prove that we are right. Ironically, the first step toward righteousness is acknowledging that we are *all* sinners.

This doesn't mean that anything goes. Jesus told the woman to "leave your life of sin" when it was all over. He was counting on the fact that loving people empowers them to live better lives. If your relationships with others are right, you find yourself doing the right thing more often. It's when our relationships are damaged that our morality becomes compromised.

As a psychologist, I couldn't agree with this more. The patients I have treated who have fallen into lifestyles that included illicit affairs got there because their relationships with others weren't right. Unhealed injuries, disappointments, or a lack of love led them down the path to destructive behavior. Simply telling them to follow the rules usually doesn't help. Loving them does.

SPIRITUAL PRINCIPLE: We are made right by being loved even when we're wrong.

SELF-RIGHTEOUSNESS

"Woe to you experts in the law . . ."
Luke 11:52

Lucy came for therapy to deal with the stress she was having in her marriage.

"He's so controlling," she explained. "I have a right to have a life, you know. After all I've sacrificed for him, you'd think he would be more appreciative."

Lucy had spent the last several years raising their children and taking excellent care of the household, and she had given up her career to do so. Now that the kids were older, she felt it was time for her to do the things she had wanted to do for years but never had the time. Lucy felt it was her turn.

"I've put up with all of his boring business parties and been involved in *everything* at the kids' school. If I were to put a price on all the things I've done for him over the years, he would find that I've saved him a fortune!"

Lucy was making a good point, but then Lucy always made good points. She was razor sharp in her reasoning, and she knew what was fair. Lucy was demanding her rights, and I could imagine that her husband was having a difficult time disagreeing with her.

Lucy dedicated herself to the raising of their children because she believed it was the right thing to do. She sacrificed herself for her husband's career because she thought that was right too. In fact, Lucy had always done what she thought was the right thing to do and never let anyone coerce her into anything. It's just that now Lucy thought that pursuing her own interests outside of the family was the right thing to do and was angry that her husband and children weren't more grateful for what she had done for them.

"The kids are old enough to take care of themselves if I want to go back to work. And if I want to go out with my girlfriends once in a while, you'd think he would be happy to see me having a good time," she grumbled.

What Lucy didn't realize was that her husband wasn't oppressing her—her need to be right was. As our sessions went on, I discovered that Lucy had always felt she was trying to do the right thing in life and that this was always being undervalued by other people. The feeling of being unappreciated was not new; it's just that now she was expressing it in a new way. Lucy was looking out for herself because she didn't believe anyone else was going to. She had given to her family for years, but she had not been receiving what she needed in exchange.

What Lucy needed wasn't to be right; it was to have the right kind of relationships. She had been doing the right things all along, but for some of the wrong reasons. As it turned out, her family did want her to pursue her own interests—they just didn't want to be left out of the process. They felt hurt that she needed to separate herself from them as if they had done something wrong. Being self-centered was not going to give Lucy what she needed. She needed to have better relationships with the people who loved her.

After many months of therapy, Lucy isn't as resentful as she used to be toward her husband. She doesn't talk as much about her rights as she used to. Instead, she is talking more about what she needs. She's working part-time because she is trying to balance her needs with the needs of her family, and she feels pretty good about that. Lucy is more satisfied with her life even though she doesn't think as much about whether she's doing the *right* thing. She now thinks more in terms of whether she's doing the *loving* thing. Lucy had fallen into the trap of narcissism and was in the process of getting herself out of it. She thought she needed to demand her rights because others didn't value her enough to meet her needs. But she isn't feeling that way as much these days, and she's sounding a lot less self-righteous at the same time.

Jesus taught that the need to be right was a sign of self-righteousness. The righteous are humble. In the biblical story of Martha and Mary (Luke 10:38–42), Martha was indignant, felt Mary was taking advantage of her, and felt justified in asking Jesus to reprimand Mary for her behavior. Sometimes demanding our rights is really self-righteousness, or in psychological terms, narcissism masquerading as justice.

The issue wasn't that Mary was doing the right thing and Martha wasn't; it was the attitude of their hearts Jesus was concerned about. Martha could have been working away in the kitchen righteously, enjoying her relationship with Jesus there. But she was so concerned about who was doing the right thing that she felt entitled to be critical of Mary for her appearance of unrighteousness. Martha was critical of Mary because Martha was concerned about herself. Self-righteousness is self-absorbed, while righteousness never loses sight of the other.

SPIRITUAL PRINCIPLE: Demanding your rights may not be meeting your needs.

THE MYTH OF INDIVIDUALISM

*"Whatever you did for one of the least of these brothers of
mine, you did for me."*
Matthew 25:40

Kyle is an independent thinker. He teaches at a junior college, is
active in his political party, and has written a few books. Some
people consider Kyle to be a little eccentric because his style of
clothing and his behavior are somewhat different from the norm,
but everyone who knows Kyle considers him to be one of the
most intelligent people he or she knows.

Kyle believes in thinking like an individual because he believes
"group think" is for the mediocre. He thinks society evolves
based upon the survival of the fittest, and he values "thinking
outside the box." For him, creativity and individuality go hand in
hand. He likes to think he is self-reliant and that he "marches to
the sound of a different drummer."

Kyle's emphasis upon individuality, however, makes him
somewhat argumentative with people because he doesn't want to
conform to what others think. He's been divorced twice because
he doesn't believe any woman can understand him. He has a hard
time with his male friends because he competes with them without even knowing it. Kyle likes to think of himself as different,
which helps him not feel so bad when he is alone.

What Kyle doesn't realize is that he needs other people in order
to feel like an individual, to think of himself as "different." Kyle is
constantly monitoring what other people do and say so that he can
reassure himself that he is not like them. Actually, Kyle is very dependent upon others in order to know who he really is. He just wants to
pretend that the opinion of the group doesn't matter to him so he
can go on defining himself as the guy who does his own thing.

What Kyle hasn't realized yet is that individuality is a myth. He
thinks, in his own mind, that he is living outside of society, but he is

just as much a part of it as anyone else. Kyle definitely has a relationship to other people—an "oppositional" one. Without people to be in opposition to, he has no way of defining himself as different.

Kyle will go on feeling frustrated in life until he comes to grips with the truth about human nature. Jesus taught that we were designed for relationships. We can go about them in billions of different ways, but we cannot escape the fact that we need them in order to be whole.

It is a frightening thing to depend on others, even God, so we turn to the myth of individualism to protect ourselves. We convince ourselves that there is no God and that all we really need is self-reliance. That way we do not have to face our fear of disappointment, which comes with trusting others. We can pretend that being right makes us righteous and that all we have to do is know the rules, or make our own, and follow them religiously to make ourselves feel safe.

Individualism is a myth, a defense against how frightening it is to truly depend upon someone other than ourselves for our well-being. No one gives us what we believe we need exactly when we want it, but we cannot achieve wholeness in isolation. Individualism is an illusion, and atheism a defense, against our fears that our fundamental need for someone outside of ourselves will only lead to frustration. Fearing that we will end up alone, we pretend that is where we wanted to be all along.

Jesus taught that we were created for the purpose of being in relationships. Our dependency is the force that drives us into relationships with God and others, where we can find the sense of wholeness. When Jesus said, "Whatever you did for one of the least of these brothers of mine, you did for me," he was driving home the psychological point that we are all connected to each other. It is only an illusion to pretend that we aren't.

SPIRITUAL PRINCIPLE: Humanity is a group experience.

YOU ARE NOT GOD

"Worship the Lord your God and serve him only."
Luke 4:8

Chloe is a tortured soul. She agonizes over every decision, constantly feels guilty, and has reduced human contact in her life to a few friends whom she rarely sees anymore. Chloe doesn't go out much because it's just too much work. She is afraid something will happen to ruin her whole day, so she's better off not even leaving the safety of her apartment.

Chloe is terrified of germs. She spends a tremendous amount of time every day cleansing herself from them. She can't just wash her hands once like other people; she has to make sure they are clean by washing them five times. Germs are the reason she won't invite anyone over to her apartment. If anyone touches something of hers, he or she will leave germs on it, and she will be forced to clean it repeatedly. Because you can't see germs, it's a lot of work for her to keep her place germfree.

Chloe suffers from an obsessive-compulsive disorder. She will get obsessive thoughts about germs contaminating her environment and then feel compelled to engage in compulsive behaviors to protect herself from them. She can't help it. Once she obsesses about germs, she compulsively has to cleanse herself of them.

Chloe doesn't realize it, but germs are not the real enemy in her life. She has had good reason to be afraid, plenty of times, but that started long before she even thought about germs. Chloe grew up as an only child in a household in which her parents fought constantly. She can remember crying herself to sleep many nights, terrified that someone was going to get hurt and her parents would end up divorced. She was very afraid that her world was going to crumble, and she had no idea what she would do then. "Please, God," she prayed nightly, "I promise to be good for the rest of my life if you only make them stop fighting."

But Chloe's parents didn't stop fighting, so over time Chloe turned to a secret world of fantasy to deal with her fears. She would imagine that if she walked home from school without stepping on a single crack, then her parents wouldn't fight that evening. Sometimes, hearing them fighting, she would imagine that if she thought about a particular word hard enough, it would make them stop. Because Chloe's parents failed to make her feel safe, Chloe had to take on that job for herself. If there were no one bigger and stronger out there to trust, then she would have to trust the magical thinking of her own mind.

Unfortunately, Chloe's fantasy that her mind had magical powers grew beyond trying to make her parents stop fighting. By the time she reached adulthood, it had expanded to a number of areas of her life in an attempt to create a sense of safety in a world that offered so little of it. Today she is mostly concerned about germs. Now she imagines that if she follows the dictates of her own mind, she will be safe from whatever danger germs pose for her. If she couldn't trust her parents, or even God, to protect her from harm, then she was forced into placing her trust in the power of her own mind.

Jesus taught that people need to worship God. Worshiping anything else simply doesn't work. We all need to feel protected, and we cannot achieve that feeling without someone bigger than us being there for us when we need it. Psychologically, we can only develop the ability to soothe ourselves if we have had someone we can trust and look up to in our development. Jesus wanted people to place their trust in God, because that is exactly what they needed to do to have a peaceful life. Who better to make us feel safe than the creator of the universe? Chloe tried worshiping the power of her own mind, and it only led to misery and fear. Jesus taught that worshiping God isn't for God; it's for us.

SPIRITUAL PRINCIPLE: Worshiping your own mind is serving too small a god.

THE KEY TO THE CENTERED SELF

"He who has been forgiven little loves little."
Luke 7:47

I believe it is important to look at the past, but I don't believe we should live there. By that I mean an unexamined life causes us to get stuck, while understanding the impact of our history on our present frees us to make different choices than we would otherwise make. Rebecca didn't understand how her childhood was robbing her of her adulthood. Paradoxically, it is by talking about our past that we can be set free from it.

Rebecca was raised in a conservative community in the Midwest where she learned traditional family values. She is grateful for her upbringing, and she loves her parents very much. The only problem she could think of when she was growing up, and she didn't even view it as a problem then, was the fact that her only sister, Sabrina, was mentally handicapped. This placed a financial and emotional burden on her parents that Rebecca knew was hard for them. She always admired their commitment and the dedicated way in which they went about caring for Sabrina.

"They were always so good," Rebecca described her parents. "I mean, I know how difficult it was for them to deal with Sabrina and all, but they never complained. I never once heard either of them talk as if they regretted one thing. My parents are amazing."

Ironically, this created a problem for Rebecca. Because she never heard her parents complain, she believed it would be wrong of her to complain as well. But she *did* have complaints about all the time and energy it took to care for Sabrina and how responsible she felt for her whenever her parents weren't around. Secretly Rebecca resented that she wasn't raised in a normal home where she could invite her friends over without having to worry about being embarrassed. Rebecca could never admit to these feelings in front of her parents, explaining, "After all, look at all they had done."

"I feel so bad. What kind of horrible person is resentful of a mentally ill sister? I mean, I was the lucky one. I got to be smart and normal, and everything. There but for the grace of God . . ."

Rebecca felt terribly guilty about feeling the way she did toward Sabrina. She thought she was a bad person for having these feelings. Rebecca's therapy forced her to face another difficult task in her life. To find healing for the painful feelings she had inside, she was going to have to forgive the hardest person there is to forgive—herself. She needed to forgive herself for resenting Sabrina, wanting more from her parents than she received, and for being the normal child. For Rebecca to love herself and others in the open and vulnerable way she wanted, she was going to have to remove the wall of guilt and resentment around her heart. Forgiving herself was the only way to do that.

The deepest form of forgiveness is a process of understanding that requires effort and a change of mind. It is rarely a one-time event, but usually the result of a series of conversations. The more we understand, the more we can change our minds and the deeper we can forgive. Fortunately, Rebecca's traditional values make her a person who works hard in her therapy, so the process of forgiving herself is going well. Just as Jesus predicted, there is a powerful relationship between feeling forgiven and the ability to love in Rebecca's life. It's just that the person she needed to forgive was herself.

Jesus taught that forgiveness is one of the most powerful tools available to humankind. Many people underestimate its psychological importance. Countless lives have been transformed over the course of human history as a result of the experience of having been forgiven. In addition to this, Jesus also taught that forgiveness benefits the forgiver. Forgiveness removes the resentments within ourselves that are an impediment to a spiritually centered life. As Rebecca discovered, it is especially true that "he who has been forgiven little loves little" when the person in need of forgiveness is ourselves.

SPIRITUAL PRINCIPLE: Sometimes forgiving yourself is the hardest act of love.

SELF-LOVE

"Love your neighbor as yourself."
Matthew 22:39

Pierre tries to be a positive role model for the students he teaches. "Kids these days need someone to look up to, and I take my job as a teacher very seriously in that way," he said proudly.

I admired Pierre for dedicating his life to helping children, and I admired him even more for coming to therapy when he started to burn out from it.

"I know my work with the kids is really important. I just need some help getting my edge back so I can keep going," he said somewhat sadly.

"Negative thinking holds us back," he informed me after one self-improvement seminar he had taken. "I just need to imagine myself as happier in order to become it. We are what we believe."

I found myself agreeing with some of what Pierre had to say on the surface, but it also seemed to me that he was leaving something out as well. His ideas about self-development focused exclusively on how he felt about himself, as if other people only held him back.

"I need to erase those parental tapes," he said about his childhood. "All that's in the past. I need to love myself and stop expecting anyone else to do that for me."

Pierre thought self-love was something he could convince himself of in spite of how he had been treated by others. His parents had neglected him as a child, so he learned early in life not to look to anyone else for what he needed. The truth was, Pierre felt unloved, and he wanted to distance himself from those feelings. Doing positive things and utilizing positive self-talk were his strategies for overcoming his painful feelings.

Unfortunately Pierre's strategy wasn't working as well as he would have liked. Because his own parents had been so devaluing of him, he struggled to avoid self-condemning feelings about himself as a result. His attempts to love himself were really attempts to quiet his inner voices of self-doubt and degradation. Pierre's problem wasn't a lack of self-love; it was the presence of self-loathing. His efforts to add the former to his life were really attempts to cover over the latter.

Over the course of our therapy Pierre has stopped trying to convince me, and himself, that self-love is merely an attitude of the mind that he can learn, like memorizing pithy phrases. Instead, we have gradually spent more time talking about what he doesn't like about himself. Yet something ironic is happening. As Pierre shares with me what he really feels about himself, he is finding that he doesn't have to cover everything over as much as he used to do. Although his parents left him with the feeling that he was worthless, the experience of being listened to when he is at his worst is giving him the feeling that perhaps there is something lovable about him after all. Pierre learned from his parents how self-hatred is tied to our relationships with others, and he is learning in therapy how self-love is too.

Pierre is happier in his role as a schoolteacher these days. He is no longer frustrated by his attempts to convince children that they need to love themselves to get ahead in life. Now he simply loves them. He has learned that it is the most powerful thing he can do for them, as well as for himself.

Jesus was very clear that his definition of self-love had nothing to do with self-absorption. To him, self-love was intimately tied to the love of others, just as self-hatred was inextricably tied to the abuse of others. When he said, "Love your neighbor as yourself," he was explaining that the love of self could not be separated out from the love of others; one was dependent upon the other.

This means that the devaluation of ourselves is hurtful for all those around us. Hating ourselves is no gift to our neighbor. This also means that the hatred of our neighbors leads to the devaluation of ourselves. Love multiplies in endless supply when it is given away, just as hatred continues to destroy as long as it is allowed to exist.

SPIRITUAL PRINCIPLE: Self-love and the love of others—one can't be done without the other.

THE CENTERED SELF IS NOT SELF-CENTERED

"You are in me, and I am in you."
John 14:20

Sometimes people wait until it's almost too late to seek help in therapy. Jake came for therapy because his wife was leaving him. They had been having marital problems for several years but had tried to work things out on their own. Jake was an outspoken, charismatic businessman, and his wife was more of an introvert. Apparently Jake was the dominant one in the relationship, and his wife had become resentful and unable to communicate her unhappiness.

"She won't even talk about it," he cried. "I've got no idea what she's thinking or feeling." Jake's wife had gone to stay at a friend's house until she could "sort things out." He was devastated. "How can she do this to the kids?"

Jake could admit that he wasn't perfect, but he didn't believe he deserved this. He thought they should try to work this out, and he thought she was being selfish by running out on him. They had both invested nine years in their marriage, and he couldn't believe this was happening.

At first Jake wanted to talk almost exclusively about his wife. The sessions were filled with his pleas for my help in getting her back. He was primarily interested in figuring her out and getting her to change her mind. Jake was in therapy to change his wife.

As time went on, Jake began to realize that he was doing in therapy what he had been doing in his marriage for the past nine years, and it just wasn't working. Jake wanted what he wanted. He wasn't a bad person, or even a particularly selfish one, but his happiness was contingent upon whether or not other people did what he wanted them to do. Jake wanted his wife to want him, but she needed to get away from him in order to find out if that was what she wanted as well. He required her to love him, but love required is not a gift worth giving.

Although it was hard for him, Jake changed the way we spent our sessions together. He took his focus off of trying to change his wife and put it on trying to understand himself. Through several painful hours Jake came to the awareness that he was trying to control others because he was afraid he might be left all alone if he didn't. It finally came out that Jake was angry about his wife leaving him because he was afraid he *did* deserve it. As Jake began to face himself, his desire to blame his wife faded. He even got to the point where he thought she should only come back when *she* felt it was the right thing to do. Although it hurt him to be abandoned by his wife, it was starting to hurt him more to think he had driven her to do it.

Thankfully, Jake's wife did return. She returned, however, to somewhat of a different man. Jake listens more when she speaks, and he tells her how he feels about what she has said. He's calmer than he used to be, his blood pressure is generally lower, and he asks his wife what she wants to do on Saturdays because he's less driven by agendas than before. Jake is more centered now because his relationship with his wife caused him to look at some painful aspects of himself he was trying to avoid. He faced his suffering, and he was able to love his wife and family in a deeper way because of it. Jake is learning the lesson that Jesus taught by example in his own life. Love is free, but it's not cheap. To truly love someone forever we must be willing to pay a price that might cost us our lives, but we become who we were created to be in the process.

Jesus did not believe that the centered self could be separate and apart from others. He said, "You are in me and I am in you" when we believe in God. He did not aspire to self-development that ignored our relationships with God and others. He aspired to love others, which was the creative force behind the spiritually centered life. To him, we could only know who we were inside

Knowing Yourself

ourselves if we knew we were loved from the outside by God. His form of spirituality was not centered on the individual self; it was centered on a relationship that took us outside of ourselves.

The reason many people try to find their sense of self apart from their relationships with others is that opening ourselves up to the love of others makes us vulnerable to getting hurt. Jesus demonstrated in his own life the profound relationship between love and suffering. Suffering is the price we pay when we enter into relationships with others, and love is the reward. Those who are willing to pay this price can find a centered self, and those who are unwilling become self-centered.

SPIRITUAL PRINCIPLE: The centered self is not self-centered.

More could be said. But time, space, and my own perspective limit me. The bridge between the teachings of Jesus and contemporary psychological theories is a solid one capable of being well traveled. I welcome the perspectives of other psychologists who would join me there. My goal here was to offer my own perspective on how the ancient teachings of Jesus contain powerful psychological insights that can benefit our lives today. For centuries, those who have been willing to contemplate on his parables have benefited from the pearls of wisdom found in them. As our ability to reflect on human behavior becomes more psychologically sophisticated, I believe that our ability to benefit from this wisdom will only increase.

Hopefully you are in a dialogue. Perhaps it is a dialogue with the words of Jesus about which you have just read. Or perhaps it is a dialogue with a therapist or healing community. But Jesus has left us with the axiom that conversation is a good thing, both with other people, and with God. It is not a good thing to be alone. This book is about a conversation between the teachings of Jesus and evolving psychological thought. I hope sitting in on the dialogue has benefited you in some way.

I realize that writing a book on the teachings of Jesus can be controversial. I have tried to leave room for other spiritual or theological interpretations of the particular sayings mentioned here. My perspective is a psychological one, which has benefited my life and the lives of my patients. Although the science of psychology is officially only a little over a hundred years old, it has been developing in the minds of many preeminent thinkers for many times that. As I think of all the ancient figures that have been referred to in modern times as "psychological" in their writings I can think of no one more deserving than Jesus of the title *The Greatest Psychologist Who Ever Lived*.

NOTES

CHAPTER 1

1. An important psychoanalytic book on how what we know is always limited by our own perspective is George Atwood and Robert Stolorow, *Structures of Subjectivity* (Hillsdale, NJ: Analytic Press, 1984).

2. I explain the "unconscious" more fully in Chapter 8.

3. "They are zealous for God, but their zeal is not based on knowledge" (Rom. 10:2).

4. Heinz Kohut, *The Restoration of the Self* (Madison: International Universities Press, 1977), p. 68.

5. Allan Bloom was a college professor who observed his students for over thirty years. He came to the conclusion that "almost every student entering the university believes, or says he believes, that truth is relative." Professor Bloom was so disturbed by this that he wrote a book to confront this destructive belief entitled *The Closing of the American Mind: How Higher Education Has Failed Democracy and Impoverished the Souls of Today's Students* (New York: Simon & Schuster, 1987).

6. Stephen Mitchell, *Relational Concepts in Psychoanalysis* (Cambridge, MA: Harvard University Press, 1988).

CHAPTER 2

1. A groundbreaking psychoanalytic book on the relational nature of the human "self" is Heinz Kohut's *The Analysis of the Self* (Madison: International Universities Press, 1971).

2. "And the Lord was grieved that he had made man on the earth" (Gen. 6:6).

3. Carl Rogers, *On Becoming a Person* (Boston: Houghton Mifflin, 1961).

4. Heinz Kohut, *How Does Analysis Cure?* (Chicago: University of Chicago Press, 1984).

5. "God created man in his own image . . . male and female he created them" (Gen. 1:27).

CHAPTER 3

1. The concept of organizing principles is explained in Robert Stolorow and George Atwood, *Contexts of Being* (Hillsdale, NJ: Analytic Press, 1992), chap. 2.

CHAPTER 4

1. The wise use of money is addressed elsewhere by Jesus. See Matthew 25:14–30.

2. More about psychopathology as self-preservation may be found in Heinz Kohut, "Introspection, Empathy and the Semi-Circle of Mental Health," *International Journal of Psychoanalysis* 63 (1982): 395–407.

3. "Godly sorrow brings repentance that . . . leaves no regret" (2 Cor. 7:10).

4. *Teleos* can be translated "reaching the end, completed, or mature."

5. *Hamartia* is the most frequently used Greek word for "sin" in the New Testament and can be translated "to miss the mark" or "be mistaken out of ignorance."

CHAPTER 5

1. More on religious rigidity in psychotherapy can be found in Mark Baker, "The Loss of the Self-Object Tie and Religious Fundamentalism," *Journal of Psychology and Theology* 26, no. 3 (1998): 223–31. Why human thinking becomes concrete is explained further in George Atwood and Robert Stolorow, *Structures of Subjectivity* (Hillsdale, NJ: Analytic Press, 1984), chap. 4, "Pathways of Concretization."

2. Sigmund Freud, "The Future of an Illusion," in J. Strachey, ed., *The Standard Edition of the Complete Psychological Works of Sigmund Freud* (London: Hogarth Press, 1927).

3. For a definition of "fundamentalist," see Mark Baker, "The Loss of the Self-Object Tie and Religious Fundamentalism."

CHAPTER 7

1. For an in-depth book on the primacy of affect in human relationships, see Joseph Jones, *Affects as Process: An Inquiry into the Centrality of Affect in Psychological Life* (Hillsdale, NJ: Analytic Press, 1995).

2. Allan Schore, *Affect Regulation and the Origin of the Self* (Hillsdale, NJ: Lawrence Erlbaum, 1994).

3. Daniel Goleman, *Emotional Intelligence: Why It Can Matter More Than IQ* (New York: Bantam, 1995).

CHAPTER 8

1. A technical discussion of transference and the unconscious can be found in R. Stolorow, B. Brandchaft, and G. Atwood, *Psychoanalytic Treatment: An Intersubjective Approach* (Hillsdale, NJ: Analytic Press, 1987), chap. 3; and R. Stolorow and G. Atwood, *Contexts of Being* (Hillsdale, NJ: Analytic Press, 1992), chap. 2.

CHAPTER 9

1. For more on the interconnectedness of human experience, see Daniel Stern, *The Interpersonal World of the Infant* (New York: Basic Books, 1985); and Stephen Mitchell, *Relational Concepts in Psychoanalysis* (Cambridge, MA: Harvard University Press, 1988).

CHAPTER 10

1. An important article on psychoanalysis and empathy is Heinz Kohut, "Introspection, Empathy and Psychoanalysis," *Journal of American Psychoanalytic Association* 7 (1959): 459–83.

2. "A wicked and adulterous generation looks for a miraculous sign" (Matt. 16:4).

3. "Because he himself suffered when he was tempted, he is able to help those who are being tempted" (Heb. 2:18).

4. ". . . on the way they had argued about who was the greatest" (Mark 9:34).

CHAPTER 11

1. A psychoanalytic book on the significance of focusing upon the relationship in therapy is Lewis Aron, *A Meeting of the Minds: Mutuality in Psychoanalysis* (Hillsdale, NJ: Analytic Press, 1996).